T0301957

An Analysis of

Richard J. Evans's

In Defence of History

Nicholas Piercey
with
Tom Stammers

Published by Macat International Ltd
24:13 Coda Centre, 189 Munster Road, London SW6 6AW.

Distributed exclusively by Routledge
2 Park Square, Milton Park, Abingdon, Oxon OX14 4RN
711 Third Avenue, New York, NY 10017, USA

Routledge is an imprint of the Taylor & Francis Group, an informa business

www.macat.com
info@macat.com

Cataloguing in Publication Data
A catalogue record for this book is available from the British Library.
Library of Congress Cataloguing-in-Publication Data is available upon request.
Cover illustration: Etienne Gilfillan

ISBN 978-1-912302-52-9 (hardback)
ISBN 978-1-912128-77-8 (paperback)
ISBN 978-1-912281-40-4 (e-book)

Notice
The information in this book is designed to orientate readers of the work under analysis,
to elucidate and contextualise its key ideas and themes, and to aid in the development
of critical thinking skills. It is not meant to be used, nor should it be used, as a
substitute for original thinking or in place of original writing or research. References and
notes are provided for informational purposes and their presence does not constitute
endorsement of the information or opinions therein. This book is presented solely for
educational purposes. It is sold on the understanding that the publisher is not engaged
to provide any scholarly advice. The publisher has made every effort to ensure that
this book is accurate and up-to-date, but makes no warranties or representations with
regard to the completeness or reliability of the information it contains. The information
and the opinions provided herein are not guaranteed or warranted to produce particular
results and may not be suitable for students of every ability. The publisher shall not be
liable for any loss, damage or disruption arising from any errors or omissions, or from
the use of this book, including, but not limited to, special, incidental, consequential or
other damages caused, or alleged to have been caused, directly or indirectly, by the
information contained within.

CONTENTS

THE MACAT LIBRARY

The Macat Library is a series of unique academic explorations of seminal works in the humanities and social sciences – books and papers that have had a significant and widely recognised impact on their disciplines. It has been created to serve as much more than just a summary of what lies between the covers of a great book. It illuminates and explores the influences on, ideas of, and impact of that book. Our goal is to offer a learning resource that encourages critical thinking and fosters a better, deeper understanding of important ideas.

Each publication is divided into three Sections: Influences, Ideas, and Impact. Each Section has four Modules. These explore every important facet of the work, and the responses to it.

This Section-Module structure makes a Macat Library book easy to use, but it has another important feature. Because each Macat book is written to the same format, it is possible (and encouraged!) to cross-reference multiple Macat books along the same lines of inquiry or research. This allows the reader to open up interesting interdisciplinary pathways.

To further aid your reading, lists of glossary terms and people mentioned are included at the end of this book (these are indicated by an asterisk [*] throughout) – as well as a list of works cited.

Macat has worked with the University of Cambridge to identify the elements of critical thinking and understand the ways in which six different skills combine to enable effective thinking.
Three allow us to fully understand a problem; three more give us the tools to solve it. Together, these six skills make up the **PACIER** model of critical thinking. They are:

ANALYSIS – understanding how an argument is built
EVALUATION – exploring the strengths and weaknesses of an argument
INTERPRETATION – understanding issues of meaning

CREATIVE THINKING – coming up with new ideas and fresh connections
PROBLEM-SOLVING – producing strong solutions
REASONING – creating strong arguments

To find out more, visit **WWW.MACAT.COM.**

CRITICAL THINKING AND *IN DEFENCE OF HISTORY*

Primary critical thinking skill: EVALUATION
Secondary critical thinking skill: REASONING

Richard Evans wrote *In Defence of History* at a time when the historian's profession was coming under heavy attack as a result of the 'cultural turn' taken by the discipline during the late 1980s and the 1990s. Historians were being forced to face up to postmodern thinking, which argued that, because all texts were the product of biased writers who had incomplete information, none could be privileged above others. In this reading, there could be no objective history, merely the study of the texts themselves.

While *In Defence of History* addresses all aspects of historical method, its key focus is on an extensive evaluation of this postmodern thinking. Evans judges the acceptability of the reasoning advanced by the postmodernists – and finds it badly wanting. He is strongly critical both of the relevance and of the adequacy of their arguments, seeking to show that, ultimately, they are guilty of failing to accept the logic of their own position. All texts are equally valid, or invalid, they suggest – while insisting that the products of their own school are in fact more 'true' than those of their opponents. Evans concludes by pointing out that this same argument could be advanced to suggest that the works of Holocaust deniers are just as valid as are those of historians who accept that the Nazis set out to commit genocide. So why, he demands, is no postmodernist willing to say as much? A devastating example of the usefulness of relentless evaluation.

ABOUT THE AUTHOR OF THE ORIGINAL WORK

Sir Richard Evans is one of Britain's most respected scholars of German history. Born in London in 1947, Evans studied history at Oxford with some of the most respected thinkers of his time, and went on to have a distinguished academic career, eventually becoming Regius Professor of Modern History at Cambridge. He made his name with publications on the history of feminism, crime, and disease in nineteenth-century Germany, before turning to write an influential trilogy on the Third Reich. Evans has also crafted himself a reputation for identifying and analyzing the misuse of history and historical ideas, specifically when it comes to Holocaust denial, and his *In Defence of History* has established itself as one of the texts most widely read by modern undergraduate historians.

ABOUT THE AUTHORS OF THE ANALYSIS

Dr Nicholas Piercey holds a PhD in cultural studies from University College, London. He is currently an Honorary Research Associate in UCL's Department of Dutch in the UCL School of European Languages, Culture & Society.

Dr Thomas Stammers is lecturer in Modern European history at Durham University, where he specialises in the cultural history of France in the age of revolution. He is the author of *Collection, Recollection, Revolution: Scavenging the Past in Nineteenth-Century Paris.* Dr Stammers's research interests include a wide range of historiographical and theoretical controversies related to eighteenth and nineteenth-century Europe.

ABOUT MACAT

GREAT WORKS FOR CRITICAL THINKING

Macat is focused on making the ideas of the world's great thinkers accessible and comprehensible to everybody, everywhere, in ways that promote the development of enhanced critical thinking skills.

It works with leading academics from the world's top universities to produce new analyses that focus on the ideas and the impact of the most influential works ever written across a wide variety of academic disciplines. Each of the works that sit at the heart of its growing library is an enduring example of great thinking. But by setting them in context – and looking at the influences that shaped their authors, as well as the responses they provoked – Macat encourages readers to look at these classics and game-changers with fresh eyes. Readers learn to think, engage and challenge their ideas, rather than simply accepting them.

'Macat offers an amazing first-of-its-kind tool for interdisciplinary learning and research. Its focus on works that transformed their disciplines and its rigorous approach, drawing on the world's leading experts and educational institutions, opens up a world-class education to anyone.'

Andreas Schleicher
Director for Education and Skills, Organisation for Economic Co-operation and Development

'Macat is taking on some of the major challenges in university education … They have drawn together a strong team of active academics who are producing teaching materials that are novel in the breadth of their approach.'

Prof Lord Broers,
former Vice-Chancellor of the University of Cambridge

'The Macat vision is exceptionally exciting. It focuses upon new modes of learning which analyse and explain seminal texts which have profoundly influenced world thinking and so social and economic development. It promotes the kind of critical thinking which is essential for any society and economy. This is the learning of the future.'

Rt Hon Charles Clarke, former UK Secretary of State for Education

'The Macat analyses provide immediate access to the critical conversation surrounding the books that have shaped their respective discipline, which will make them an invaluable resource to all of those, students and teachers, working in the field.'

Professor William Tronzo, University of California at San Diego

WAYS IN TO THE TEXT

KEY POINTS

- Richard J. Evans is a British historian, born in 1947, famed for his work on imperial and Nazi Germany,* and his writings on historical method (that is, methods of research and analysis in the academic field of history).

- Written in the context of the mistrust of "objective* truths" and traditional Western historical methods typical of postmodernist* beliefs, *In Defence of History* (1997) offers a robust defense of the pursuit of accuracy and neutrality in the process of researching, writing, and studying history.

- In this work of historiography*—roughly, the study of the methods and aims of historians—Evans charts the development of history as a scholarly practice; employing examples from his own research, he demonstrates that history still has a distinct place among the social sciences.

Who Is Richard J. Evans?

Richard J. Evans, the author of *In Defence of History* (1997), is one of the foremost historians of Germany working in Britain today. Born in the north-east London suburb of Woodford in 1947, he studied history at Oxford University with some of the greatest historians of the time, and developed an interest in historical methodology. He was particularly drawn to the historian E. H. Carr's* seminal work *What Is*

History?, a text whose influence is clearly evident in his own writing. Evans decided to specialize in German social history,* inspired by the controversy around Fritz Fischer,* a historian who held Germany responsible for the outbreak of World War I.* Holding lectureships at Stirling University, the University of East Anglia, and Birkbeck College (University of London), Evans published highly acclaimed studies on German feminism,* criminal justice, and public health.

While teaching at Birkbeck, Evans decided to publish *In Defence of History*, alarmed at the growth and implications of postmodern approaches to analysis within the historical profession; postmodernism is a movement relevant to contemporary arts and cultural analysis, usually characterized by a disbelief in objectivity and the sense that all interpretations are equally valid. As a historian concentrating on modern Germany, Evans recognized the potential danger in this framework. While he had previously written specifically on German historians wrestling with the Third Reich* (the regime created by Adolf Hitler* and the Nazi Party in 1933 that lasted until the end of World War II* in 1945), *In Defence of History* was the first time Evans addressed broader questions of historical method.

His expertise on Nazism led to his appointment as a witness in the Irving*–Lipstadt* libel case, in which the British author David Irving unsuccessfully sued the American historian Deborah Lipstadt for libel; Evans's testimony was pivotal in exposing Irving as a denier of the Holocaust* (the industrial extermination of many millions of European Jewish people by Nazi Germany during World War II).

In 2008 Evans was appointed as Regius Professor of History at the University of Cambridge and used his inaugural lecture to champion the tradition of previous British historians who had written about continental Europe (published as *Cosmopolitan Islanders* in 2005). Author of an acclaimed recent trilogy charting the rise and demise of the Third Reich, Evans has been awarded numerous honors, including the presidency of Wolfson College, Cambridge, and a knighthood from the Queen in 2012.

What Does *In Defence of History* Say?

In Defence of History is Evans's attempt to confront the dangers posed by postmodern theory to the practice of history.

The debate about whether history could ever be a science with identifiable laws and the ability to predict future outcomes, and whether it could lay claim to objectivity—the belief that it is possible to identify "real" phenomena regardless of personal prejudices—was not new. Indeed, Evans was keenly interested in how this question had been debated in the 1960s by the British historians G. R. Elton* and E. H. Carr. But the existing skepticism about historical method had been placed on a new footing due to the impact of emerging ideas about language, sometimes referred to as the linguistic turn* in critical theory, articulated by literary critics and philosophers such as the French thinkers Roland Barthes* and Jacques Derrida.*

These theorists suggested that the meanings of words are not fixed to the objects or ideas to which they refer but, rather, that they function through their difference from, and relation to, words and other signifiers—such as sounds and images—that point us towards meaning. Historical events, then, could not be seen to have a single, fixed meaning or single interpretation. Building on these insights, thinkers and academics such as the historian and cultural critic Hayden White* suggested that historical writing was not radically dissimilar to literature, since different historians could examine the same piece of evidence and draw different conclusions and interpretations. The British postmodern historian Keith Jenkins* went further and argued that documentary records are necessarily incomplete and never really impartial, making it impossible for historians to use documents in order to gain access to the "truth" about the past.

This observation struck at the heart of history as a discipline–throwing into doubt its methods, its purpose, and its intentions to tell the truth.

Evans aimed to refute the postmodern challenge on multiple fronts. First, by re-describing the development of the historical discipline, he showed that debates around objectivity, selection of source material, and politics of representation were not new; history as a discipline had often been more diverse, more self-critical, and more radical than its postmodern enemies liked to purport. Second, he maintained that postmodernists' claims about texts and language were internally inconsistent on a conceptual level, and threatened to delegitimize their own practice (that is, that postmodern assumptions were not secure in themselves, and might jeopardize the very ability of historians to work toward sound analysis). Third, Evans argued that postmodern skepticism toward the possibility of objectivity carried unexpected social and political consequences. He recognized that if there were no standard for judging truth or accuracy, this opened the door to a variety of distorted or reactionary ideas, including Holocaust denial.

It is important to note that the primary focus of his attack was not postmodern philosophers, but those historians who had cited these ideas in an attempt to overhaul how history was written.

Evans's fundamental strategy for refuting the postmodernists' position on truth, causation, and objectivity involved grounding his counterarguments in practical examples rather than abstract linguistic theory. His defense of the pursuit of objectivity was welcomed at a time when many academic historians feared that postmodernism threatened to completely undermine the idea of shared methods and rules of evidence within the discipline. Although both orthodox and postmodern commentators criticized it, the book was a commercial success; 12 editions have been published to date, and it has been translated into several European and Asian languages. The history of its reception reveals a great deal about the ongoing development of how and why historical research is conducted.

In Defence of History remains an ideal introduction to the methodological controversies—that is, disputes concerning the ways in which historical research and analysis is conducted—that raged in the field at the end of the twentieth century.

Why Does *In Defence of History* Matter?

While the work is not revolutionary in its thought, what sets *In Defence of History* apart is its ability to provoke thought about how history is practiced, and the way in which it informs readers about a broad range of thinkers and historians, from traditional empiricists* (that is, those who believe in the authority of knowledge founded on evidence that can be verified by observation) to postmodernists. The work maps the evolution of the discipline since the 1960s to encompass many types of social history (that is, roughly, historical studies that focus on all sections of society). Evans also draws on his personal research into modern German history to illustrate his own approach. His ability to discuss complex and wide-ranging issues in a simple and engaging manner makes his means of expression almost as important as the ideas contained within the work, countering the opaqueness of postmodern theory with a grounded, approachable rhetorical style. His commitment to objectivity does not restrain him from providing an often very subjective, critical account of his peers; *In Defence of History* also offers a showcase of lively, even notably forceful, argument.

In addition, Evans's public profile, and his numerous appearances as an expert on issues of historical memory and the legacy of Nazism, demonstrate the relevance of his approach far beyond the academic world. Evans's involvement in the Irving–Lipstadt trial highlighted the grave importance of producing an accurate and verifiable version of past events. In his subsequent writings he has reflected further on the public and civic function of historians, showing how scholarship can inform popular understandings of the past.

While questions remain about the way Evans conceives objectivity, subjectivity (that is, interpretation influenced by personal feelings or assumptions), and causation in history, *In Defence of History* has, as the reviews indicate, provoked and widened debate. The substantial and combative Afterword that accompanies the editions from 2000 onward shows how many vital questions of method and of ethics were raised by Evans's intervention. The fundamental issue at stake is the question of whether an objective historical truth is desirable or even conceivable. Evans succeeded in arguing convincingly that, while subjectivity will surely play a role in historians' interpretations, objectivity remains worth pursuing.

SECTION 1
INFLUENCES

MODULE 1
THE AUTHOR AND THE
HISTORICAL CONTEXT

KEY POINTS

- *In Defence of History* remains one of the most influential and lucid accounts of historical method to appear in the past generation.
- Evans had emerged as an esteemed social historian,* allowing him to comment authoritatively on recent historical trends.
- Evans was writing against the backdrop of the breakdown of classic Marxist* interpretations—that is, interpretations founded on the analytical methods of the political theorist and economist Karl Marx*— and new pressures on the institutions of higher education.

Why Read This Text?

Based on a series of lectures, Richard J. Evans's *In Defence of History* was published in September 1997. The title reflects a justifiable anxiety arising from the intellectual landscape in the late 1980s and early 1990s; in particular, it attempts to defend the practice of history from what Evans sees as the threat of extreme postmodernism* (a movement in the arts and cultural analysis that has questioned long-established assumptions in fields such as literature and the social sciences) and the challenge that postmodern ideas pose to concepts of scholarly objectivity,* the neutrality of facts, and the scientific nature of history.

In the work, Evans attempts to demonstrate the vitality of history as a means for accessing the past, while also defending the importance of rigorous historical methods. Evans notes that in the mid-1990s,

> **❝** In this sense, the problem of how historians approach the acquisition of knowledge about the past, and whether they can ever wholly succeed in this enterprise, symbolizes the much bigger problem of how far society can ever attain the kind of objective certainty about the great issues of our time that can serve as a reliable basis for taking vital decisions for our future in the twenty-first century. **❞**
>
> Richard J. Evans, *In Defence of History*

academic history had seen a serious challenge from postmodern thinkers, including the historians Keith Jenkins* and Hayden White* and the philosopher of history Frank Ankersmit.*

Evans provided a concise and influential account of how historical methods had evolved. He argued that historians were indeed capable of finding out the "truth" about what happened in the past, even if this truth was always partial and provisional. Evans stirred up a great deal of controversy—so much so that *In Defence of History* prompted widespread reflection about what, if anything, historians could learn from postmodernism.

Author's Life

Richard J. Evans is a career historian. He was born in Woodford, a suburb of London, in 1947, the son of a teacher at a nearby school.[1] His parents had migrated to London from a small Welsh village during the early twentieth-century economic downturn known as the Great Depression.*[2] Evans went to study Modern History at Jesus College, Oxford, in 1966. While studying at Oxford, Evans came into contact with the ideas of English Marxist historians (historians following the analytical assumptions of the political theorist and economist Karl Marx), the *Annales* school* (a deeply influential school of historians associated with the study of sections of society beyond men and women of high status), and the radical group involved with the *History Workshop Journal**[3] (a circle of historians who shared something of the aims and methods of both the Marxist and the *Annales* historians). He attended lectures by noted historians Christopher Hill,* Keith Thomas,* and Hugh Trevor-Roper.* In 1969, Evans graduated with a first-class honors degree before moving to St Antony's College, Oxford, to complete his doctoral degree with research on the feminist* movement in Germany in the early twentieth century.

Following his studies, Evans held lectureships at the University of Stirling and the University of East Anglia. Between 1989 and 1998, Evans was professor of history at Birkbeck College, University of London, where he wrote *In Defence of History*, published in 1997. He was Regius Professor of Modern History at the University of Cambridge from 2008 to 2014.

Politically, Evans can be considered to be broadly center-left and was influenced by Marxist and left-wing ideas during his time at university.

Evans is best known for his works on Nazi Germany* and the Holocaust,* including his *Third Reich Trilogy*[4] and his study of postwar German historiography* *In Hitler's Shadow*.[5] In 2000, Evans was involved as an expert witness for the defense in a legal case brought by the British author David Irving* against the American historian Deborah Lipstadt,* who had named Irving as a Holocaust denier.[6] This experience demonstrates the practical importance of Evans's stance on truth and objectivity in historical analysis, one which insists that not all interpretations are equally valid—as the specific case of Holocaust denial clearly shows—and that historical evidence can be deployed to establish the facts of an event.

Author's Background

The late twentieth century saw a dynamic debate about the role of history in contemporary academia, with some scholars even proposing the wholesale dissolution of history as a discipline. During the 1980s and 1990s, a strand of postmodernism criticized traditional ideas about the authority of knowledge, particularly the prominence of the Western point of view, going as far as to advocate a *relativist** position, in which it is impossible for any historian to establish a single, objective "truth" about the past.

Although these views were uncommon among practicing historians, radical skepticism flourished among theorists of history and historiography. Drawing on French thinkers such as the literary theorist Roland Barthes,* the social theorist Michel Foucault,* and the philosopher Jacques Derrida,* the 1980s and 1990s saw a marked advance of critical theory within the humanities, accompanied by the political and ideological shift occurring at the end of the Cold War* (the long period of tension between the United States and its allies and the communist Soviet Union* and its allies, which began following World War II* and ended in the last decade of the twentieth century).

At the same time, many of postmodernism's defining features, such as a mistrust of grand narratives that purport to offer universal truths about the world, displaced the primacy of Marxism, an analytical method and political position that had previously provided the governing framework for many social historians.

This intellectual shift was linked to a wider realignment in higher education. Although history departments—and the total number of practicing historians—expanded rapidly in the 1960s and 1970s, this trend was reversed in the 1980s when right-wing governments came to power in Britain and the United States and cut funding to universities. This setback saw academic historians suffer a drop in their pay, independence, and status, and—according to Evans—the profession threatened to fragment into many disparate fields.[7] In their rejection of the idea of objective truth, postmodernists claimed that historians tended to propagate versions of the past that suited the needs and reflected the values of those in power and neglected the perspectives of marginalized people. Evans strongly disagreed with the more extreme, totalizing views of postmodernists towards history as a discipline, but he did acknowledge that the debate about how history is researched, written, and taught had distinct merit and value in 1990s Britain.[8]

NOTES

1   Information on Richard J. Evans's career can be found via his personal website, http://www.richardjevans.com.

2   Daniel Snowman, "Daniel Snowman Meets the Historian of Germany, Defender of History and Expert Witness in the Irving Trial," *History Today* 54 (2004): 45.

3   Richard J. Evans, "Review: *The Annales School: An Intellectual History* by André Burguière," London Review of Books 31, no. 23 (2009): 12–14.

4   Richard J. Evans, *The Coming of the Third Reich* (London: Allen Lane, 2003); *The Third Reich in Power, 1933–1939* (London: Allen Lane, 2005); *The Third Reich at War 1939–1945* (London: Allen Lane, 2008).

5   Richard J. Evans, *In Hitler's Shadow: West German Historians and the Attempt to Escape from the Nazi Past* (New York: Pantheon Books, 1989).

6   Debra Lipstadt, *History on Trial: My Day in Court with David Irving* (New York: HarperPerennial, 2006).

7   Richard J. Evans, *In Defence of History*, 2nd ed. (London: Granta, 2001), 171–3.

8   Evans, *In Defence of History*, 179, 205.

MODULE 2
ACADEMIC CONTEXT

KEY POINTS

- Historical theory and historiography* (the study of the aims and methods of historians) both consider the evolution of the discipline of history.

- Conservative "positivist"* historians tended to argue that historians can reconstruct the past accurately through studying documents; by contrast, those influenced by the intellectual current of postmodernist* thought denied that objective knowledge of the past was possible since all historians interpret their sources through the lens of their own cultural preoccupations, assumptions, and biases.

- Richard J. Evans tried to steer a course between the two, arguing that although a degree of subjectivity (roughly, the impossibility of conducting analysis without bias) on the part of historians is inevitable, documentary evidence can provide verifiable facts that helpfully constrain interpretations of past events.

The Work in its Context

Richard J. Evans's *In Defence of History* was aimed primarily at those postmodernist thinkers who had questioned the relevance of history as a discipline through a fundamental challenge to notions of authoritative readings of past events and the concept of objectivity.* In the early nineteenth century, history had been placed on a more rigorous, scientific footing thanks to the teachings of the German historian Leopold von Ranke.* Ranke insisted that through scrupulous examination and comparison of archival materials,

> ❝ The theory of history is too important a matter to be left to theoreticians. Practicing historians may not have a God-given monopoly of pronouncing sensibly on such matters, but they surely have as much right to try and think about them as anyone else; and the experience of actually doing historical research ought to mean that they have something to contribute which those who have not shared this experience cannot offer. ❞
>
> Richard J. Evans, *In Defence of History*

historians would be able to view the past "as it really was." Ranke and his supporters generally believed in the primacy of political and diplomatic history, and devoted their studies to understanding the behavior and decisions of statesmen.[1] A significant number of nineteenth- and twentieth-century scholars, however, believed that historians should pay as much attention to social groups beyond the ruling elite, to economic patterns, and the wider canvas of cultural life.

Some of the issues raised by the intellectual movement of postmodernism—such as the distorting role of the historian, or the unreliability of narrative—may have seemed novel but are actually many centuries old. "Two and a half thousand years ago," Evans observes, "the Greek historian Thucydides* complained in the preface to his history of the Peloponnesian War that poets and others were purveying false and imaginary accounts of what had happened, and announced his intention of setting the record straight."[2] The postmodern challenge in the 1980s was distinct, though, because its attack on historical objectivity—roughly, the possibility of arriving at "truth" in historical analysis—was linked to new theories of language. Many postmodernist thinkers insisted that words (or "signifiers") derive their meaning from their relation to, and difference from, other words rather than through a fixed relation to objects and concepts in the world. Influenced by French thinkers like Roland Barthes* and Michel Foucault,* postmodernists argued furthermore that meaning is generated by the reader; what the reader finds in a text, then, is far more important than the author's intention.

They argue that truth can never be absolute or universal, but is always partial or contingent (that is, dependent on certain assumptions or perspectives), and historical documents—like any other texts—are open to infinite interpretations. Evans wrote *In Defence of History* to show the danger of such views for historians.

Overview of the Field

Evans took the unusual step of beginning *In Defence of History* with reference not to recent postmodern thinkers but to the debates of an earlier generation. The German British historian G. R. Elton* and the British Marxist historian E. H. Carr* had outlined radically different views of historical method in the 1960s, with Elton endorsing the unmediated authority of historical documents, and Carr rejecting empiricism*—the idea that arguments should be founded on evidence certified by observation, and not through theory—in favor of history that recognized the interplay between archival evidence and present-day preoccupations. Despite their differences in outlook, Evans clearly admired both men. Unlike the postmodern historian Keith Jenkins,* who wrote about historical method in the abstract, Carr and Elton had honed their philosophical insights out of the experience of working with archives and documents.

We can broadly divide the scholars who write on questions of historical method into three groups. The first could be seen as a traditional, yet shrinking, group of empiricists like Elton. They believed in the possibility of reaching objective knowledge about the past through immersion in historical documents. The second group could be considered a broad majority of historians, including Carr and

Evans, who believed, to different extents, that access to the past through historical research was possible but that this would always be fragmented, incomplete, and informed by the contemporary concerns of the historian. A third, newer group of theorists, the postmodernists, which included the Dutch historian Frank Ankersmit* and Jenkins, broadly believed that history could not provide an objective, disinterested account of past realities. For the postmodernists, historical writing is a construct of the dominant group in the present.

Academic Influences

In Defence of History was directly modeled on E. H. Carr's classic 1961 volume *What Is History?* Evans borrowed many of his chapter headings from Carr, and the last paragraph of the book is a "parody of Carr's final paragraph."[3] Carr's main influence on Evans's historiographical thinking was his assertion that history is a dialogue between past and present. It is not constructed solely from documentary evidence, nor entirely from the agenda of the historian, but arises from the interplay between the two. Carr also wanted to broaden the remit of historical research beyond the elite classes and world leaders. Yet Evans also offers a critique of an element of hypocritical selectivity in Carr's work, stating that Carr was "absolutely clear that those who had (in his view) contributed little or nothing to the creation of historical change as he saw it, such as women, or the pre-literate and politically unorganized masses, were not really deserving of the historian's attention."[4]

In addition, Evans was concerned about the teleological* assumptions in Carr's thinking (that is, his assumptions that history can be thought of as a procession of events towards a specific end). As a Marxist* apologist for some of the policies of the Soviet president Joseph Stalin,* a ruler noted for his brutality and ruthlessness, Carr had a strong sense of historical necessity, seeing some violent actions as defensible if these acts furthered the progress of society. Carr thought the only developments worth writing about were those that succeeded in disrupting the present or changing the future. Evans recognized that such thinking had "extremely disturbing" implications, since it could lead the historian to turn away from telling the story of defeated causes or marginalized groups.[5]

In the same way, Evans did not agree with all of Carr's rather determinist* understanding of causation (that his, his idea that certain events were inevitable, given the prevailing circumstances), his support for models imported from the social sciences, or his belief in historians' powers of prediction.[6] While an admirer of Carr, Evans also strives to demonstrate the ways in which he is different from his predecessor.

NOTES

1 Richard J. Evans, *In Defence of History*, 2nd ed. (London, Granta, 2001), 16–19.

2 Evans, *In Defence of History*, 260.

3 Evans, *In Defence of History*, 269

4 Evans, *In Defence of History*, 212.

5 Evans, *In Defence of History*, 269–70.

6 Evans, *In Defence of History*, 138, 73.

MODULE 3
THE PROBLEM

KEY POINTS

- In the late twentieth century, practicing historians and critical theorists—roughly, thinkers working in the intersection of philosophy, literature, and the social sciences—questioned how well history could provide an objective and true account of the past, and whether this was possible at all.

- Postmodern* literary critics believed that texts could refer only to other texts; transferring this principle to history, postmodern thinkers such as the historians Hayden White* and Keith Jenkins* claimed that that historical writing only referred to the historian and the present.

- Evans retold the history of the discipline using examples from his own historical practice in order to make a case for the continuing value of history and of the pursuit of objectivity in writing about the past.

Core Question

Richard J. Evans's *In Defence of History* engages with fundamental questions about subjectivity—the impossibility of conducting historical analysis without influence from the historian's social context and personal biases. To what extent can history be considered objective* and true? How connected is the practice of writing about history to the object of its study, the past? In essence, these questions explore whether historians are capable of capturing and representing what actually occurred, or whether they are engaged in an exercise that reveals much more about their own present-day imagination and cultural context than past events. This issue is crucial to the validity of

> 66 For present reality can be felt and experienced by our senses; but the past no longer exists, it is not 'real' in the same sense as the world around us in the present is real. It too has become a text. 99
>
> Richard J. Evans, *In Defence of History*

history as a field of study and research discipline. If, as some postmodernists suggest, the past is irrecoverable, then the concept of history as a study of the past becomes impossible and the discipline in its current form is finished. The idea of objectivity, truth, and accuracy are fundamental concepts for historians, and *In Defence of History* sets out to uphold the claim that historians can and should seek the truth about the past, even if this truth is only ever partial.

While these debates were a prominent aspect of the rise of postmodern thinking in the late twentieth century, such issues were not entirely new. As Evans observes, the possibility of a scientific or objective history was central to the formation of the discipline in the nineteenth century. In the 1960s, the empiricist* historian G. R. Elton* and the relatively radical Marxist* historian E. H. Carr* clashed over competing visions of how historians worked and what they could know. The answers given by Carr and Elton could not hold up when, in the 1980s, new forms of postmodern theory emerged and became fashionable within new philosophies of history and historiography.*

Informed by the "linguistic turn"* in philosophy and critical theory, which emphasized the role of language in all forms of cultural analysis, postmodernists challenged the basic premise of historical documents as transparent or referring to objective, external phenomena; rather, they suggested that history was inherently subjective, constructed in the mind of the historian and reflecting historians' cultural contexts. Postmodernist ideas did encourage a broader and more inclusive approach to presenting and interacting with historical evidence, which Evans duly acknowledges.[1] But he felt obliged to write *In Defence of History* in order to combat what he saw as some of postmodern philosophy's more dangerous possible implications, such as a disregard for rigor, blatant partisanship by the author, and moral relativism* (roughly, the position that moral judgment is not really possible since we cannot truly be certain of anything in matters of morals).

The Participants

The intellectual origins of the postmodern challenge to history can be seen in the literary criticism that appeared from the late 1960s. In France, theorists of language such as Roland Barthes* and Jacques Derrida* undermined conventional ideas about language and meaning. In Barthes's essay "Death of the Author" (1977), he dismissed the idea that readers can fully decipher or recover an author's original intention. For Barthes, meaning is secured through the act of reading and interpretation and not established definitively by authorial intention.[2] Barthes also noted that conventional historians believed that the past was waiting to be discovered, while Barthes viewed historical narratives as an "effect" created by literary and scholarly strategies.[3]

Similarly, the intellectual movement known as deconstruction* emphasizes the theory that our knowledge of the world is entirely mediated by language. As Derrida and other deconstructionists assert, meaning emerges out of the interplay between linguistic signs; therefore nothing can be imagined to exist "outside the text" and the reader's interpretation, not the author's intention, is the place where meaning is ultimately generated.[4]

These ideas were expanded upon and applied to history by the historians Hayden White, Frank Ankersmit,* and Keith Jenkins.

Hayden White noted that history is a construct, like all literature, and is governed by a similar reliance on narrative. For White, within the confines of the historical method there are multiple, equally viable, ways of representing the past.[5] Jenkins observed that history is a discourse—that is, very roughly, a system of statements and assumptions making up a "text"—situated within a particular ideology; rather than attempt to study the past, Jenkins contended that historians should only study what other historians have said.[6] Like White, Ankersmit proposed that history is a construct, and the differences between historical works cannot be explained by research but by style.[7] Rather than study the past itself, history should focus on how the past is represented in the present.

These postmodern ideas fundamentally question the purpose and validity of history. *In Defence of History* is an attempt to rehabilitate the notion that historical texts are fundamentally connected to reality and that the principles of rigorous research, impartiality, and objectivity are still worth pursing for the practicing historian.

The Contemporary Debate

Evans resented the dismissive comments made about historians by postmodern thinkers, particularly those whose own publications displayed very little use of rigorous historical method. To refute their indictments, Evans drew extensively on the ideas of his predecessors, including an examination of the clash between Elton and Carr in the 1960s, going as far back as the British historian G. M. Trevelyan,* who was a pioneering practitioner of social history* in the late nineteenth and early twentieth centuries.

In Defence of History seeks to rebut the postmodern notion of history as essentially defunct by providing a more persuasive account of how the historical profession developed in the nineteenth and twentieth centuries. His demonstration of the range of topics covered and approaches used by historians convincingly undercuts the attempt by postmodernists to caricature historians as a single group with an elitist agenda. Using a balance of light wit and assertive argument, Evans cites debates on the techniques of nineteenth-century historians to debunk the supposed novelty of several postmodernist recommendations, such as the demand for historians to pay more attention to oppressed groups: "When a postmodern historian argues in the mid-1990s for a 'rediscovery of history's losers', one wonders what planet he has been living on for the last 30 years."[8] In tackling complex philosophical notions like objectivity, Evans drew on contemporary American debates featuring historians such as Peter Novick* and Thomas Haskell* regarding the subtle difference between objectivity and neutrality.

Evans approaches the central concept of objectivity by providing numerous examples of historical theory and highlighting famous controversies among scholars—for instance the 1950s dispute between the British historians Lawrence Stone* and Hugh Trevor-Roper* over Stone's interpretation of documentary evidence regarding the status of the seventeenth-century English aristocracy, and the 1980s debate over the controversial link drawn by the American historian David Abraham* between big business and the rise of Hitler.*[9]

NOTES

1   Richard J. Evans, *In Defence of History*, 2nd ed. (London, Granta, 2001), 248.

2   Roland Barthes, "The Death of the Author," in *Image, Music, Text* (London: Fontana, 1977), 142–8.

3   Evans, *In Defence of History*, 94.

4   Jacques Derrida, *Of Grammatology*, trans. Gayatri Chakravorty Spivak (Baltimore, MD, and London: Johns Hopkins University Press, 1997); and Evans, *In Defence of History*, 94–5.

5   Hayden White, *Metahistory: The Historical Imagination in Nineteenth-Century Europe* (Baltimore, MD, and London: Johns Hopkins University Press, 1975); and Evans, *In Defence of History*, 100–1.

6   Keith Jenkins, *On "What Is History?" From Carr and Elton to Rorty and White* (London: Routledge, 1995); and Evans, *In Defence of History*, 97.

7   F.R. Ankersmit, *Historical Representation* (Stanford, CA: Stanford University Press, 2002).

8   Evans, *In Defence of History*, 213.

9   Evans, *In Defence of History*, 116–23.

THE AUTHOR'S CONTRIBUTION

KEY POINTS

- Evans was inventive in addressing head-on the postmodern* challenge that objectivity* in historical research was impossible by showing through historical practice that some form of objectivity was desirable and possible.
- Evans attacked the political pretensions of postmodernism, by drawing on his own previous work on the Holocaust.*
- He offered an inclusive overview of the profession and showed the benefits and dangers of postmodernism.

Author's Aims

Richard J. Evans's *In Defence of History* engages directly with the criticisms coming from postmodernist thought. While some practicing historians thought that these arguments were not worth rebutting, Evans felt that this was complacent, in light of how influential such arguments were in undergraduate courses. Evans states unequivocally that the "theory of history is too important to be left to the theoreticians"[1] and sets out to persuade his readers "that it [is] possible to defend history as an intellectual undertaking by genuinely confronting and arguing with the extreme skeptics rather than by simply ignoring them or covering them with abuse."[2]

In his argument against extreme postmodernist views, Evans attempts to demonstrate inherent contradictions within postmodern concepts as well as the dangers of adhering to an extreme relativism,* a position in which any version of the past is a valid as any other.

Readers who expect a detailed dismantling of postmodern philosophy may also misunderstand the book's aims. While Evans

> ❝ Yet drawing up the disciplinary drawbridge has never been a good idea for historians … Historians should approach the invading horde of semioticians, poststructuralists, New Historicists, Foucauldians, Lacanians and the rest with more discrimination. Some of them might prove more friendly, or more useful, than they seem at first sight. ❞
>
> Richard J. Evans, *In Defence of History*

wishes to counter extreme postmodern theory, he only does so in relation to the practice of history and not by making bigger philosophical interventions. One aim of *In Defence of History* was to narrate the phases through which the historical profession had developed, from the primacy of political history, through to the expansion of economic, social, and cultural history in the 1960s and 1970s. In doing so, Evans showed that historians were much more self-conscious about their own approach than their critics alleged. To illustrate this point he drew on examples from his own research. For instance, to respond to the postmodernist historian Hayden White's* argument that history is essentially a literary form, Evans relates how his own major book *Death in Hamburg* had been organized around "twelve parallel narratives" for "aesthetic" reasons, in order to present the material in "the most exciting and the most interesting way" while also being based in rigorous examination of historical fact.[3] For Evans, it is simply untrue that historians are naive, or unwilling to reflect on their active role in constructing stories about the past.

Approach

Evans connected to specific social and political outcomes the philosophical question about whether objectivity was possible for historians. He rejected the claim made by the British postmodernist historian Keith Jenkins* that historians are simply involved in reproducing dominant values through institutions, particularly the university. He does this by documenting many instances of historians—especially those in social history*—who had explicitly set out to reveal injustices in the past and document the plight of oppressed groups, such as the working classes, women, and sexual minorities.[4]

Meta-narratives* of historical change—that is, roughly, accounts offering very broad perspectives on historical currents, suggesting that history is moving in a certain direction—are by no means inherently reactionary (that is, opposed to social progress), as he argues by reference to Marxism* and feminism* (the activism and theory of those advocating equality between the sexes). By extension he also questioned whether postmodernism was really as progressive and radical as it liked to pretend. Finally, Evans asks: if postmodernism alleges there are no objective grounds for deciding between different versions of history, beyond moral or aesthetic preference, then does it "give a license to anyone who wants to suppress, distort or cover up the past?"[5]

The force of Evans's critique came from his background in German history. During the 1980s a fierce dispute known as the *Historikerstreit** ("historians' quarrel") saw historians clash over the uniqueness of the Holocaust, by comparison with the policies of mass murder in other regimes, and the difficulties of reconstructing or morally understanding Nazi* crimes. Evans was a close observer of this debate, and in an article in the *Journal of Modern History* he set out his belief that social history could play a useful role in gaining a moral understanding about this period.[6] The debate made clear to Evans the stakes of the discussion about objectivity—and the dangers of insinuating, like some postmodernists did, that any version of the past was as good as any other.

Contribution in Context

In Defence of History, like E. H. Carr's* *What Is History?*, originated as a series of lectures given by the author.[7] Evans notes that he developed his ideas on historical knowledge, objectivity, and truth during his time at the British institution Birkbeck College in the 1990s. His arguments belong to the historical mainstream, and are close in many respects to other important writers on historical practice in the 1990s, such as the British historians John Tosh* and Ludmilla Jordanova.* Evans is careful to establish that he is not writing in defense of any one school, but, rather, championing a diversity of approaches to the past. Against those traditionalists such as G. R. Elton* or the American historian Gertrude Himmelfarb,* who had linked the defense of objectivity with a call for a return to elitist political history, Evans celebrates the widening of topics tackled by historians since the 1960s and 1970s. Evans's commitment to shared methods of verification accompanies a call for "a little intellectual tolerance" for the many different kinds of historical research.[8]

Unlike traditionalists such as Elton, who were hostile to social history, Evans sees many positive elements in the contemporary developments. New opportunities for trade and exchange were creating an "international marketplace of ideas" and a boom in interest in world history.[9] Evans's account of postmodernism is by no means entirely negative; its emphasis on the importance of narrative and style, for instance, has helped "reinstate good writing as a legitimate historical practice," as seen in the imaginative work of cultural historians such as Robert Darnton* and Natalie Zemon-Davies,* author of the bestselling *The Return of Martin Guerre*, in the 1980s.[10] Evans welcomes elements of postmodern thinking that were already compatible with long-running historical self-scrutiny, or could be beneficially assimilated into historical practice. *In Defence of History* is aimed at demolishing the more destructive elements of postmodernism, which threatened to explode any concept of truth in history.

NOTES

1   Richard J. Evans, *In Defence of History*, 2nd ed. (London: Granta, 2001), 14.

2   Evans, *In Defence of History*, 255.

3   Evans, *In Defence of History*, 146.

4   Evans, *In Defence of History*, 20–68.

5   Evans, *In Defence of History*, 232–3.

6   Richard J. Evans, "The New Nationalism and the Old History: Perspectives on the West German *Historikerstreit*," *The Journal of Modern History* 59, no. 4 (1987): 761–97.

7   Daniel Snowman, "Daniel Snowman Meets the Historian of Germany, Defender of History and Expert Witness in the Irving Trial," *History Today* 54 (2004): 47.

8   Evans, *In Defence of History*, 182.

9   Evans, *In Defence of History*, 177.

10 Evans, *In Defence of History*, 244.

SECTION 2
IDEAS

MODULE 5
MAIN IDEAS

KEY POINTS

- Evans's primary aim is to defend an idea of weak objectivity* in historical practice, presenting history as a "weak" rather than "hard" science.

- Historical method is a crucial means for establishing what really happened in the past; while historians can never establish the truth of the past absolutely, they can approximate it through examining documents with professional rigor.

- Evans wrote in a deliberately clear and entertaining way, in order to contrast with the jargon used by his postmodern* enemies and to connect with a general reader.

Key Themes

In the introduction to *In Defence of History*, Richard J. Evans outlines the debate concerning the current state of the discipline and notes that some extreme postmodernists have questioned the validity of history and its future as a field of study. Here, Evans indicates that the central purpose of the book is to defend history from such criticisms and make the case for saving it. He does this through reviewing the evolution that the discipline has undergone in modern times.

While recognizing the importance of the nineteenth-century historian Leopold von Ranke,* an early champion of analytical archival research, Evans charts how notions of objectivity developed as historians began to favor an expanding variety of source material such as diplomatic dispatches, government minutes, and statistical records.[1] A social historian* by background, Evans welcomed the widening of

> **❝** The language of historical documents is never transparent, and historians have long been aware that they cannot simply gaze through it to the historical reality behind. Historians know, historians have always known, that we can only see the past 'through a glass, darkly'. It did not take the advent of postmodernism to point this out. What postmodernism has done is to push such familiar arguments about transparency or opacity of historical texts and sources out to a set of binary opposites and polarized extremes. **❞**
>
> Richard J. Evans, *In Defence of History*

the historical agenda in the 1960s to include documentary evidence from overlooked and excluded groups, combining the values of Ranke with the aims of progressive politics and a global history perspective.[2] *In Defence of History* is strongly grounded in Evans's commitment to thinking historically about the practice of history itself. He alleges that one of the weaknesses of postmodern historians is their unwillingness to engage in the "self-reflectivity" about their own position that they recommend to others, showing that one of the key faults of the postmodern critique of history is that the relativism* it espouses can easily be used to undermine its own position.[3]

Evans answers the claim that the inherent subjectivity of history prevents it from ever being scientific by asserting that that history is a "weak" science, unlike hard sciences such as physics, chemistry, and biology—areas of study governed by precise laws which permit a high degree of predictability in experimental settings. Elaborating on his interpretation, Evans insists that it is "always a mistake for a historian to try and predict the future. Life, unlike science, is simply too full of surprises."[4] While history is not based on laws that would allow historians to reliably predict the future, it has standards, methods, and a body of knowledge that make its practice scientific. It also produces generalizations about the past that can be tested. Evans outlines that history is a mix of science, art, and craft.[5] He shows that at their best, historians do not simply reproduce society's dominant ideas but have the power, through a commitment to rigor and accuracy, to, "punctur[e] the clichés of popular historical myth."[6] When practiced fairly and thoroughly, history allows us to approach the truth of what happened in the past, even if this truth will always be approximate— "tenable though always less than final."[7]

Exploring the Ideas

Evans believes that some form of objectivity is possible because documents are connected to the reality of the past, and by comparing and examining them, historians can decipher which sources are reliable and illuminating. Document-based historical practice places limitations on what historians can realistically say about past events, and Evans believes postmodern theorists are wrong to insinuate that historians are free to invent or construct what happened. He also concedes, however, that historians will bring their own ideas to their research and cannot be totally independent of their cultural context. He echoes the Marxist* historian E. H. Carr* in claiming that historians "do not just listen to the evidence, they engage in a dialogue with it, actively interrogating it and bringing to bear on it theories and ideas formulated in the present."[8] With this core concept, Evans maintains that history is a valid discipline with persistent relevance.[9]

In making his points, Evans draws heavily on issues arising out of historical practice, grounding his assertions on these concrete examples rather than abstract theorizing. In reviewing the debate between G. R. Elton* and E. H. Carr on the subject of methods of research and analysis, he connects their philosophical outlook with their historical research. Elton advanced an empiricist* claim that historical documents, and the facts they contain, would speak for themselves; Evans exposes a blind spot in Elton's historical practice, suggesting that his unwillingness to consider the role of present-day context leaves a number of his own biases unacknowledged. A key example of this is the preference for strong government in the period of British history known as the Tudor era (1485–1603), which Evans believe reflects Elton's contemporary concerns.[10] Conversely, Carr believed that the historian's job was to look back from the vantage point of the present to identify what factors and events had contributed most to the progress of humanity. His own Marxist beliefs led him to equate "objectivity" with writing in defense of the progressive cause of the Soviet Union.*

While there are benefits to the transparent acknowledgment of a scholar's own political position, there is a danger that it can over-determine the historian's treatment of their subject matter—that is, it can bear too much influence. In Evans's view, Carr's left-wing politics made his historical writing intolerant to any groups who had opposed the Russian Revolution of 1917, in the course of which the Tsar, the nation's ruler, was overthrown and a communist government was imposed.[11] These examples demonstrate how Evans sought to move beyond older, flawed definitions of objectivity while answering the postmodern challenge by showing what lessons can be learned from studying historical practice.

For Evans, an objective historian is both imaginative but confined by the limits of the evidence available for examination, while also resisting the intrusion of his or her own political or moral stance. While histories of the past will only ever be provisional, incomplete, and guided by external theories from the present, objectivity lies in the suspension of historians' own moral or political agenda in the selection and analysis of their source material.[12]

Language and Expression

Evans's work is lucidly written and engages with a wide range of sources and ideas. Because the text emerged from courses he taught at Birkbeck College in London, it was intended to serve as an introduction to major issues in the discipline, such as facts, causation, and objectivity in as clear and accessible a manner as possible.[13] Beyond the desire to achieve maximum accessibility and transparency, his writing style represents a strategy to highlight the difference between himself and the postmodernists who, in his view, "have developed a new level of specialized language and jargon, borrowed largely from literary theory, which has rendered their work opaque to anyone except other postmodernists." Evans seized on the obscure and inaccessible writing of the postmodernists as proof of their "narcissism" and "elitism."[14]

While welcoming the postmodernist attentiveness to how words are used, Evans recommends that historians "stick to a plain style unless they are very sure of what they are doing," since every point they make should be in the "service of clarification rather than obfuscation."[15] Evans takes pleasure in showing up the clumsiness or confusion that results from historians misusing language. Indeed one of the pleasures of Evans's prose comes from the cruel humor with which Evans pounces on his targets. The book is often irreverent towards some of the great names in the history of the profession, including Hugh Trevor-Roper* (citing his offensive comments about the "unrewarding gyrations of barbarous tribes" in Africa) and the early twentieth-century historian G. M. Trevelyan* (noting his "paternalistic and condescending stance towards [people of low social status] in history").[16] Evans is particularly unforgiving in showing up the sloppiness of his postmodern critics. For instance, in replying to the criticisms of the American historian Joyce Appleby,* he observes that "it is symptomatic of her scholarly standards that she even managed to misquote the book's title."[17] Such frank and biting asides help make the book a compelling read.

NOTES

1 Richard J. Evans, *In Defence of History*, 2nd ed. (London: Granta, 2001), 110–11.

2 Evans, *In Defence of History*, 196–8.

3 Evans, *In Defence of History*, 115.

4 Evans, *In Defence of History*, 62.

5 Evans, *In Defence of History*, 66.

6 Evans, *In Defence of History*, 207.

7 Evans, *In Defence of History*, 253.

8 Evans, *In Defence of History*, 230.

9 Evans, *In Defence of History*, 73.

10 Evans, *In Defence of History*, 230–1.

11 Evans, *In Defence of History*, 226–8.

12 Evans, *In Defence of History*, 239.

13 Evans, *In Defence of History*, 257.

14 Evans, *In Defence of History*, 200.

15 Evans, *In Defence of History*, 69.

16 Evans, *In Defence of History*, 163, 178.

17 Evans, *In Defence of History*, 256.

MODULE 6
SECONDARY IDEAS

KEY POINTS

- Evans claimed that the intellectual movement of postmodernism* has brought some benefits to the writing of history but points out the dangers of exaggerating the role of individuals and personal subjectivities (that is, roughly, biases brought about by personal beliefs and historical context, for example).

- The continuing expansion and diversification of historical research threatened to undermine the idea of history as a single discipline—but Evans was optimistic about the continuing relevance of common standards.

- For Evans, postmodern thought is more applicable to some periods and problems than to others.

Other Ideas

Richard J. Evans's *In Defence of History* is particularly concerned with the implications of postmodernism for social history.* The influence of the "linguistic turn"*—an increased focus in many areas of cultural analysis on the importance of language to the understanding of "truth"—has brought greater prominence and visibility to marginalized groups within mainstream historical writing. As a social historian whose early research interests centered on the experiences of women and criminals in nineteenth-century Germany, Evans welcomed this aspect of postmodernist influence on historical practice.[1] Like the postmodernists, he deplored the insularity and Eurocentric* arrogance of an earlier generation of scholars[2] (that is, the narrow-mindedness and the assumption that historical research

❝ To search for a truly 'scientific' history is to pursue a mirage. Insofar as it has succeeded in generating new methods and techniques, this quest has of course been enormously beneficial ... History is not only a science in the weak sense of the word, it is, or can be, an art, in the sense that in skillful hands it can be presented in a literary form and language that achieves comparability with other literary works and is widely recognized as such. ❞

Richard J. Evans, *In Defence of History*

was founded on European perspectives). He also recognized that postmodernism had helpfully emphasized the importance of ordinary individuals in history. He cited the dictum of the influential nineteenth-century political theorist Karl Marx* that "people make their own history, but they do not do it under circumstances of their own choosing."[3]

But while postmodernism had certainly helped social history develop, nuancing some of the clumsy older Marxist* models, Evans pointed out its potential for misuse. Its insights could be "pushed too far," leading to a situation where "we get an intellectual reductionism instead of a socio-economic one."[4] In other words, he thought postmodernism threatened to make the role of individual interpretation beyond reproach, neglecting the role of a wider social context and shared cultural truth.

A related danger came from the excessive importance attached to issues of personal identity. Postmodern historians were far too willing to speak as "I," openly invoking their own experiences and perceptions in describing the past, and valorizing the central role of empathy.[5] "The ultimate implication indeed is that no one can know anything beyond their own bodily identity. Experience is the sole arbiter of truth."[6] For Evans such a view was dangerous, since it suggested that only women could write the feminist* history, or only French historians should write the history of France. This position was unsatisfactory, since it deprived the oppressed of the opportunity tell the story of their oppressors, and disguised the extent to which writing good history means engaging with the "obviously other" as well as "the seemingly familiar."[7]

Exploring the Ideas

In order to demonstrate his view that postmodernists have presented a caricature of historians, Evans provides his own account of the state of the discipline. He shows how the profession has expanded massively since the 1960s, with the foundation of many new university departments. This expansion accompanied the fashion for social history and led to growing attention to groups and individuals who had previously been overlooked by mainstream historians.[8] This was a marked advance on the models of social history espoused by an older generation of historians. For instance, E. H. Carr,* despite his own work on the Russian Revolution, still suggested that the masses were only important enough to merit attention in historical writing when they were politically organized and advancing the cause of progress.[9]

Such narrow attitudes had now been overturned, and there had been a flourishing in women's history, black history, gay history, microhistory, and cultural history. Evans welcomes this democratization within historical thought. "Virtually everything of meaning or importance to contemporary humanity now has a written history and that means everything of importance to all kinds of people, not just to a small educated élite of the educated and powerful."[10]

Still, this expansion was not without its hazards. The initial hopes that social history could provide an overarching form of "total history" collapsed, as a host of subfields and subspecialisms developed. If each subfield had its own research questions and priorities, it became harder and harder to believe that there was a single historical discipline. Peter Novick,* a scholar noted for his theory of history, felt that history had fragmented so much that there was no longer a single scholarly community with its own norms and purposes.[11] Evans, however, was more optimistic. Electronic communication and frequent flights had made it easier for scholars from different parts of the world to share ideas. Moreover, although the theories historians used had diverged, this made it all the more important that they upheld common ways of referencing and presenting evidence. Contrary to the doubts of postmodernists, Evans insists, "interpretations really can be tested and confirmed by an appeal to the evidence … it really is possible to prove that one side is right and the other is wrong."[12]

Overlooked

Evans deploys his expertise on German social history to show the serious consequences of viewing all interpretations as equally valid. Following a discussion of how postmodernity can be used to justify Holocaust* denial, Evans suggests that, like other new approaches to history, postmodernist theory may be more applicable to some areas of history than others.[13] Evans believes that theories that ignore the concept of the truth in relation to the Holocaust trivialize Nazism* and its victims. He quotes Jane Caplan,* principally a scholar of Germany's Nazi history, who claimed that postmodernism cannot be used so cavalierly when it is a question of the recent suffering and deaths of many people.[14] Although Evans suggests that it is inappropriate to use postmodern theory to consider the Holocaust, he does not ask the wider question: do certain theories or methods of history fit better with particular historical periods or historical events?

It is a question that has important implications. If postmodernist theory is not appropriate for discussing the Holocaust, are there other periods or subjects to which postmodernist ideas cannot be applied? If so, what criteria can we use to establish this, and to which other theories or historical periods is this applicable? Does this just relate to the sources available to the researcher, or to the morality of the event in question?

This subtle conceptual point, however, was lost amidst those critics who felt more angered at how their comments on historiography* had been associated with Holocaust denial. In Evans's defense, his reference to Holocaust denial was predictable in light of the controversy in the 1980s surrounding the rediscovery of the wartime anti-Semitism* of the Belgian literary critic Paul de Man,* a controversy that exposed the "exculpatory implications" of his deconstructionist* theories[15] (that is, it exposed the possibility that his anti-Jewish sentiments might have informed his theoretical arguments, since it was possible to use his theory to question the "truth" of documented, and terrible, historical events).

NOTES

1   Richard J. Evans, *The Feminist Movement in Germany 1894–1933* (London: Sage Publications, 1976); *Rituals of Retribution: Capital Punishment in Germany 1600–1987* (Oxford: Oxford University Press, 1996).

2   Richard J. Evans, *In Defence of History*, 2nd ed. (London, Granta, 2001), 178.

3   Evans, *In Defence of History*, 189.

4   Evans, *In Defence of History*, 186.

5   Evans, *In Defence of History*, 200.

6   Evans, *In Defence of History*, 211.

7   Evans, *In Defence of History*, 214.

8   Evans, *In Defence of History*, 162, 171.

9   Evans, *In Defence of History*, 164.

10 Evans, *In Defence of History*, 165.

11 Evans, *In Defence of History*, 176.

12 Evans, *In Defence of History*, 128.

13 Evans, *In Defence of History*, 243.

14 Evans, *In Defence of History*, 242–3.

15 Evans, *In Defence of History*, 234.

MODULE 7
ACHIEVEMENT

KEY POINTS

- Evans succeeded in advancing a case for the importance of history and the pursuit of objectivity;* *In Defence of History* reached a large audience and was a commercial success in many countries.
- The book was also met with fierce criticism from adherents of postmodernism.*
- Evans's writing style is clear and engaging, and grounded in examples of history in practice.

Assessing the Argument

Richard J. Evans's *In Defence of History* largely accomplishes its aims. While the text has received much criticism from both traditional and postmodern thinkers for its content, Evans succeeds in outlining a personal view of why history is a valid field and why it should be defended; this work has become a standard historiographical* text for undergraduate students in many universities, particularly in the United States and the United Kingdom. Issued in hardback in 1997 and paperback in 1998, the book was quickly translated into Italian, German, Swedish, Turkish, Japanese, and Korean. Reviewers broadly agree that this work is comprehensive and convincing, but it is also a text about methodology that is surprisingly entertaining, not least because of the author's skill in skewering his opponents. As the journal *Kirkus Reviews* noted, Evans "brings colleagues, quick or dead, left or right, north or south, into the ring and merrily wrestles many to the ground."[1]

In the 2000 edition, Evans claims that "stimulating debate was one

> 66 It is right and proper that postmodernist theorists and critics should force historians to rethink the categories and assumptions with which they work, and to justify the manner in which they practice their discipline. But postmodernism is itself one group of theories among many, and as contestable as all the rest. For my own part, I remain optimistic that objective historical knowledge is both desirable and attainable. 99
>
> Richard J. Evans, *In Defence of History*

of the book's principal aims," and in this, too, he was certainly successful.[2] In Evans's recollection, the sheer amount of coverage the book received was extraordinary, arousing "far more comment than I expected."[3] Challenges to Evans's methods and conclusions came from so many quarters and ideological positions that he spent several years replying to them individually through the Institute of Historical Research online forum before answering the criticisms in print by publishing the Afterword to the 2000 edition.

Achievement in Context

In Defence of History was directly shaped by the intellectual climate in British universities in the late twentieth century. It was written in the wake of what Evans saw as the disarray and "impotence" of the academic left, "underlined by the crisis of academia which began in the 1970s and reached its height in the 1980s."[4] Evans provided a way of understanding postmodernism as a product of these transitions, and reassured fellow scholars that it would soon settle into more of a subfield or subspecialism of history "rather than revolutioniz[ing] its theory and practice as a whole."[5] Although it is linked to a specific time and place, the broad scope of the book and its central theme—

related to a universal question about historical validity—remains useful for students, teachers, and the wider public.

A cornerstone of Evans's position is his assertion that the treatment of historical material has important implications beyond academia. Notably, Evans served as an expert witness in the historian Deborah Lipstadt's* libel defense against the Holocaust*-denier David Irving* in 2000. Lipstadt was described in *In Defence of History* as the "leading authority" on Holocaust denial, and Evans echoed her concerns that conspiracy theories and "revisionism" (challenges to historical orthodoxy) had flourished in the United States in the 1990s when "attacks on the Western rationalist tradition have become fashionable."[6] During the trial he was asked to comment on the historical accuracy of Irving's work. Evans condemned Irving, showing how Irving's account of the Holocaust failed the test of honest and faithful scholarship, legitimizing Lipstadt's accusations. For Evans, it was futile to make excuses for Holocaust denial by invoking postmodern theories. "Auschwitz* was not a discourse," Evans insists. "It trivializes mass murder to see it as a text."[7]

Limitations

Although *In Defence of History* could have been useful in other subjects where postmodern ideas have provided a challenge to existing ideas and conventions—such as literary studies, art, economics, linguistics, architecture, and philosophy—Evans does not engage at length with the philosophy of postmodern thinkers. For many, this failure to analyze the views of his opponents fully is a major weakness of the text. The English literary critic Stefan Collini,* writing in the *Guardian*, complained that the book was superficial in its analysis, featuring "vulgarized rebuttals of vulgarized ideas."[8] Yet Evans turned this criticism into a compliment: "If by vulgarized, he means 'popularized', then I gladly plead guilty."[9] He was not writing for those who were experts in the realm of theory, but those who were engaging with these concepts on a practical level as an extension to their research, and lay readers without access to the specialized and sometimes opaque language used by postmodern thinkers. His hatred of postmodern jargon explains Evans's desire to translate these complex debates into more accessible language and challenge them in more transparent terms. Yet Collini's insight that Evans's desire to be popular came at the expense of any serious engagement with postmodern philosophy can still be considered valid.

Unsurprisingly, academics within those disciplines such as literary studies, which were more compatible with deconstruction* (an approach to cultural analysis that states, very roughly, that meaning is dependent on language) and postmodernism, complained that Evans had not engaged sufficiently with the theorists he was criticizing. Catherine Belsey,* a respected interpreter of contemporary philosophy, accused Evans of extolling the virtues of close reading, yet in practice misquoting and misunderstanding complex writers like the philosopher Jacques Derrida* and the literary theorist Roland Barthes.* For Belsey, Evans sacrificed real engagement with these thinkers, preferring to present his antagonists as a series of "bogeys" or "intellectual monsters to frighten the credulous."[10]

NOTES

1   "Richard J Evans—In Defence of History," *Kirkus Reviews*, November 1, 1998, accessed July 23, 2015, https://www.kirkusreviews.com/book-reviews/richard-j-evans/in-defence-of-history/.

2   Richard J. Evans, *In Defence of History*, 2nd ed. (London, Granta, 2001), 316.

3   Evans, *In Defence of History*, 254.

4   Evans, *In Defence of History*, 198.

5   Evans, *In Defence of History*, 203.

6   Evans, *In Defence of History*, 241.

7   Evans, *In Defence of History*, 124.

8   Stefan Collini, "The Truth Vandals," *Guardian*, December 18, 1997, 15.

9   Evans, *In Defence of History*, 256.

10 Catherine Belsey, "In Defence of History," *European Journal of English Studies* 3, no. 1 (1999): 108.

MODULE 8
PLACE IN THE AUTHOR'S WORK

KEY POINTS

- Evans's historical practice largely deals with modern Germany, although he has gone on to provide broader interventions on historical method.

- *In Defence of History* draws heavily on his background with the social history* of Germany, and informs his later profile as a public historian.

- More recently, Evans expands his position against nationalist histories in *Cosmopolitan Islanders* (2005), a study of the traditions of European historical practice in twentieth-century Britain.

Positioning

In Defence of History was published in September 1997, when Richard J. Evans was 50 years old and had already produced a number of historical works, primarily concerned with modern German history. As a student in Oxford he had taken a particular interest in the controversy surrounding the work of Fritz Fischer,* a historian who placed responsibility on the Germans for the outbreak of World War I.*[1] Evans developed a passion for social history, providing a significant contribution to this area with his first book *The Feminist Movement in Germany 1894–1933* (1976).[2] His major work *Death in Hamburg* (1987) dealt with the social and political implications of cholera outbreaks in the city between 1830 and 1910,[3] while *Rituals of Retribution* (1997) considered the use of capital punishment in Germany between 1600 and 1987.[4]

❝ Total relativism provides no objective criteria by
which fascist and racist views of history can be falsified
… The increase in scope and intensity of the Holocaust
deniers' activities since the mid–1970s has among
other things reflected the postmodern intellectual
climate, above all in the USA, in which scholars have
increasingly denied that texts had any fixed meaning,
and have argued instead that the meaning is supplied
by the reader, and in which attacks on the Western
rationalist tradition have become fashionable. **❞**

Richard J. Evans, *In Defence of History*

This background in German social history was fundamental to *In Defence of History*, and allowed Evans to illustrate his opposition to the implications of postmodernism* in relation to the study of the Holocaust.* While postmodernists maintain that conventional history is always the story of "the winner," often neglecting the narratives of marginalized groups, Evans regards this generalization as a myth, noting that "it is precisely the poor and the unknown, the losers and indeed, the female, who have attracted the largest number of historians and been the subject of the greatest number of books."[5] Since *In Defence in History* was published in 1997, Evans has increasingly moved away from the study of late nineteenth-century Germany to produce an important trilogy on Nazi Germany.*[6] But he has continued to make interventions on historiographical* issues that have reached not just other historians of Germany but all members of the discipline. As part of his appointment as Regius Professor of History at Cambridge, Evans delivered his inaugural lectures in 2009 on the theme of British historians of the European continent—a tradition to which he has made a notable impact.[7]

Integration

During the 1970s, Evans was one of a number of young British social historians who posed a challenge to the established view of Wilhelmine Germany* (1871–1918).[8] British social historians like Evans helped effect a shift in focus away from the consideration of high politics, the state, and Prussian dominance over other German states to include more complex social relations.[9] The group was influenced by the "New Left,"* an intellectual movement concerned with examining "history from below"[10] (that is, conducting research on individuals and communities previously considered to be inconsequential). Part of Evans's approach to history was to highlight "the importance of the grassroots of politics and the everyday life and experience of ordinary people."[11] Undermining the view that postmodernism provided a novel intervention on behalf of the oppressed, Evans makes it clear within *In Defence of History* that social history as it was already being practiced took up the mission to expose "fundamental structures of inequality in society."[12]

German history also exemplified for Evans why doing history fairly was a matter of civic responsibility. He had participated in the *Historikerstreit** (the "historians' quarrel" provoked by conservative historians who wanted to challenge the "guilt" felt by many German people) and hence observed how politically sensitive scholarly questions related to objectivity* and empathy could be. *In Hitler's Shadow* (1989) saw Evans tackling the awkwardness many German historians felt in coming to terms with the legacies of the Nazi regime, once again highlighting their potential as scholars to shape public debate.[13] This view informed *In Defence of History*, since Evans feared that postmodernism threatened to undermine historians' social obligations to seek and represent the truth; he applied this in his role as an expert witness in the libel trial lost by the Holocaust-denier and author David Irving* in 2000. The following year he reflected on the case to draw wider lessons about historians in the public sphere for his book *Telling Lies about Hitler*.[14]

Significance

The continuing influence of *In Defence of History* can still be noted in many university reading lists, and the book is currently in its 12th printing. It has also been translated into 12 languages—clear evidence of its relevance outside the United Kingdom. Despite the large volume of criticism the work received from both traditionalist and postmodern historians, Evans has done little to modify his position. In fact, he addresses his critics directly in a scathing Afterword appended to the book's 2000 edition. While the work remains less respected by scholars than his earlier research on social history—such as the classic *Death in Hamburg*—it is undoubtedly the book by Evans that has been most widely read and most hotly debated. His introduction to the fortieth anniversary edition of E. H. Carr's *What Is History?* in 2001 celebrates the work's continuing resonance.[15]

The postmodern challenge that seemed so threatening in the 1990s largely receded in the following decade. But some of the positions Evans opposes in *In Defence of History* have recurred. Evans was bitterly critical of intellectual nationalism, attacking G. R. Elton's* assumption that historians should concentrate on writing the history of the nation-state they happen to live in. Evans lamented that historians in Germany and France had generally proven to be "obstinately insular"—that is, inward-looking—when it came to studying other cultures. By contrast, Evans hailed the contribution of British and American scholars who had written momentous historical works on other countries.[16]

This theme was revived in his 2009 book Cosmopolitan Islanders. Here Evans praises the success of those English-speaking scholars who combine deep research with readability and skill in writing, and warns against the potential of a new intellectual isolationism resulting from the decline of teaching foreign languages in schools.[17]

NOTES

1   Daniel Snowman, "Daniel Snowman Meets the Historian of Germany, Defender of History and Expert Witness in the Irving Trial," *History Today* 54 (2004): 45.

2   Richard J. Evans, *The Feminist Movement in Germany 1894–1933* (London: Sage Publications, 1976).

3   Richard J. Evans, *Death in Hamburg: Society and Politics in the Cholera Years, 1830–1910* (Oxford: Clarendon Press, 1987).

4   Richard J. Evans, *Rituals of Retribution: Capital Punishment in Germany 1600–1987* (Oxford: Oxford University Press, 1996).

5   Richard J. Evans, *In Defence of History*, 2nd ed. (London, Granta, 2001), 212.

6   Richard J. Evans, *The Coming of the Third Reich* (London: Allen Lane, 2003); *The Third Reich in Power, 1933–1939* (London: Allen Lane, 2005); *The Third Reich at War 1939–1945* (London: Allen Lane, 2008).

7   Richard J. Evans, *Cosmopolitan Islanders: British Historians and the European Continent* (Cambridge: Cambridge University Press, 2009).

8   Theodor S. Hamerow, "Guilt, Redemption and Writing German History," *The American Historical Review* 88, February (1983): 65–70.

9   Richard J. Evans, "Introduction: Wilhelm II's Germany and the Historians," in Richard J. Evans, *Society and Politics in Wilhelmine Germany* (London: Croom Helm, 1978), 11–39.

10 Hamerow, "Guilt, Redemption and Writing German History," 70.

11 Evans, "Introduction: Wilhelm II's Germany and the Historians," 22–3.

12 Evans, *In Defence of History*, 212.

13 Richard J. Evans, *In Hitler's Shadow: West German Historians and the Attempt to Escape from the Nazi Past* (London: I.B. Tauris, 1989).

14 Richard J. Evans, *Telling Lies about Hitler: The Holocaust, History and the David Irving Trial* (London: Verso, 2001).

15 See E.H. Carr, *What Is History?* Introduced by Richard J. Evans (Basingstoke: Palgrave, 40th anniversary ed., 2001).

16 Evans, *In Defence of History*, 179–81.

17 See A.W. Purdue, "Book of the Week: Cosmopolitan Islanders," *Times Higher Education*, July 9, 2009, accessed October 24, 2013, http://www.timeshighereducation.co.uk/407279.article.

SECTION 3
IMPACT

MODULE 9
THE FIRST RESPONSES

KEY POINTS

- The most potent critique of Evans's position regards his view of objectivity* and the pursuit of truth—concepts the postmodernists* wished to expose as outdated.

- Critics of *In Defence* came from both traditional empiricists* and postmodernists; Evans replied by accusing his critics of being politically motivated, and showed how they in turn had misunderstood his arguments.

- This was a significant quarrel between academics, with clashes of personality sometimes taking greater prominence than the philosophical debate.

Criticism

Richard J. Evans's *In Defence of History* was intended to navigate a middle course between a traditional empiricist approach to history and the challenge of postmodern theories to the validity of the discipline—approaches with different understandings of the possibility of discovering objective truth through historical research. His work came under a great deal of scrutiny from both camps, though it had an essentially favorable reception.

Among Evans's more politically motivated critics was the conservative historian Niall Ferguson.* In Ferguson's view, history did not need defending, as it was more popular in British educational institutions than ever. Ferguson insists that the work is "rude" to historians of a "broadly conservative nature."[1] Evans's central concerns and approach to social history,* which grew out of his position within the "New Left"* in his early academic career, seem fundamentally

> ❝ I have been taken aback by the sheer variety and
> by the utterly contradictory nature of the responses
> which the book has elicited. I would not have thought
> it possible for a single book to be read, or misread, in so
> many different ways. ❞
>
> Richard J. Evans, Afterword to *In Defence of History*

incompatible with the Ferguson's broadly right-wing stance.[2]

Postmodernists criticized Evans's refusal to engage with postmodern philosophy in its own terms, misunderstanding and misrepresenting their field of thought as well as individual thinkers. Furthermore, many insisted that *In Defence of History* promoted an outdated concept of objectivity, defending conservative approaches to history, and advancing contradictory arguments. Particularly fierce criticism was leveled by the historian Keith Jenkins,* who is a key target of Evans's intellectual attacks. In *Why History?*, Jenkins devotes a chapter to Evans's work, noting that his defense of history is part of a conservative, bourgeois structure, and that his work is intended to defend not history itself, but Evans's own position in academia within a "History Club."[3]

Further critiques provoked by Evans's work were quite diverse. For instance, the American historian Joyce Appleby* suggests that Evans's argument is entirely unnecessary, seeing the postmodern rejection of the pursuit of objective truth in historical practice as too untenable to warrant so much attention.[4] Lynn Hunt,* an American scholar noted for her work in the theory of history, criticizes Evans for his constant references to outmoded debates between scholars such as G. R. Elton* and E. H. Carr.*[5] The scholar Anthony Easthope,* noted for his interest in contemporary literary theory, uses Evans's final paragraph, based on Carr's final paragraph in *What Is History?*, as evidence of a fundamental agreement with empiricist objectivity.

Responses

Evans responded to his critics in detail through the website of the Institute of Historical Research, London, between 1998 and 1999; these responses formed the basis for an Afterword which has appeared in editions of the work since 2000.

Evans convincingly defends against most critiques of his work. While he acknowledges Easthope's point about a few factual errors, he refutes other critics and accuses many of misreading his work. According to Evans, Jenkins ascribes views to Evans that he doesn't hold (and mistakenly characterizes all historians as a homogeneous elite), depicting Evans's stance on objectivity as traditionally empiricist.[6] While Evans notes the importance of some of the nineteenth-century German historian Leopold von Ranke's* method in research, throughout the book he asserts his belief in a limited objectivity in which the subjectivity of the historian plays an integral part.[7]

Diane Purkiss,* a postmodern historian notable for her work in gender and witchcraft, had accused Evans of holding conservative views and misrepresenting her work.[8] Defending his treatment of individual historians like Ferguson and Purkiss, Evans noted that he only used the words of the authors themselves, representing them fairly in his book. He argued that throughout the book he is clearly in favor of diversity and plurality in history, including some postmodern ideas. The work is intended to defend the links between the practice of writing history and the accurate representation of the past, not any particular school.

Conflict and Consensus

Evans admitted that he had made the odd "howler" in his treatment of a philosopher or theorist.[9] Yet in general he held his ground, and stubbornly pointed out the almost "comical" way that his book had been misread or misunderstood.[10] Evans insisted that his postmodern enemies had become "so angry" precisely because he had exposed their sham political posturing, and carefully detailed each of the ways in which they had misrepresented or willfully twisted his arguments.[11] Some of the phrases that infuriated them, such as the description of postmodernists as "intellectual barbarians," were left in the manuscript by Evans because "I didn't believe anyone would be stupid enough" to take the expression literally.[12] Such bad-tempered and derisory exchanges meant that there was little reconciliation between Evans and his critics.

The debate often touched on personal invective and academic rivalry, rather than clarifying important philosophical points. Doug Munro,* a scholar noted for his work in historical biography, comments, in a generally positive review, that while Evans plausibly defends himself from accusations of adherence to Elton's views on national history or gender history, these have nothing to do with his view on objectivity, which is sometimes unclear.[13] Similarly, Evans's position on causality is weak, and his adherence to many of Carr's ideas is an area that can be questioned. As Jenkins noted, Evans did not answer how causation works in practice and how one can successfully select a hierarchy of causes.[14]

The wide criticism from different quarters suggests that a consensus has not been reached on this popular work. This is perhaps to be expected; *In Defence of History* aims to refute a number of important and contradictory schools of thought and offers Evans's critical analysis of the work of individuals.

NOTES

1   Niall Ferguson, "History Is Dead, Long Live History!," *Sunday Times*, September 21, 1997.

2   Richard J. Evans, *In Defence of History*, 2nd ed. (London: Granta, 2001), 261.

3   Keith Jenkins, *Why History? Ethics and Postmodernity* (London: Routledge, 1999), 106–12.

4   Joyce Appleby, "Does It Really Need Defending?," *The Times Literary Supplement*, October 31, 1997: 10.

5   Lynn Hunt, "Does History Need Defending?," *History Workshop Journal* 46, December (1998): 241–9.

6   Evans, *In Defence of History*, 277–85.

7   Evans, *In Defence of History*, 271–2

8   Diane Purkiss, "A Response to Richard J. Evans," *History in Focus*, accessed October 24, 2013, http://www.history.ac.uk/ihr/Focus/Whatishistory/purkiss1. html. See also Diane Purkiss, *The Witch in History: Early Modern and Twentieth-Century Representations* (London: Routledge, 1996).

9   Evans, *In Defence of History*, 292.

10 Evans, "Afterword" to *In Defence of History*, 270.

11 Evans, "Afterword" to *In Defence of History*, 285.

12 Evans, *In Defence of History*, 296.

13 Doug Munro, "*In Defence of History* (Review)," *Journal of Social History* 36, no. 1 (2002): 242–4.

14 Jenkins, "On Richard Evans" in *Why History?*, 105.

MODULE 10
THE EVOLVING DEBATE

KEY POINTS

- Evans's work is regarded by some as an important but now superseded contribution, and some worry that his arguments endorse hostility to contemporary theoretical approaches to cultural analysis.

- Evans's writing on the history of historians belongs to a wider trend of studying the growth of the discipline, and considering its social role.

- The text has had a huge impact on undergraduate courses; elements of postmodern* theory such as attention to style and self-reflexivity (an awareness of the role of the researcher in the process of analysis) on the part of authors have largely been assimilated into the profession.

Uses and Problems

Richard J. Evans's *In Defence of History* can be seen as a work that not only engaged in the debate about history, but also spread the debate to a new audience inside—and beyond—professional academia. Since its publication, Evans's book has been noted in other works, such as the British historian John Tosh's* *Why History Matters* (2008) and Ludmilla Jordanova's* *History in Practice* (2006).[1] These books provide a useful introduction for students into historiographical* debates, although their approach is less polemical and argumentative, as the challenge from postmodernism seems less urgent, beyond the particular flashpoints such as Holocaust* denial.

Tosh and Jordanova are open to theoretical approaches, and want to distance themselves from the perceived conservatism of Evans's case

❝ Like other new approaches to history, therefore, postmodern theory would seem to be more applicable to some areas of history than others. A recognition of this likelihood is the first step in the direction of harnessing its more positive ideas to the research and writing of history in the twenty-first century. ❞

Richard J. Evans, *In Defence of History*

for objectivity.* Tosh dismissively remarked in his 1999 review that Evans is speaking from "somewhere near the dead center of the profession," espousing an argument that would be endorsed by "the overwhelming majority" of fellow historians. Tosh is clearly disappointed by the work's "surprising conservative" conclusions in light of Evans's previous reputation at "the cutting edge of social history."[2] Indeed, for those historians who believe in the benefits of engaging with theory, there were anxieties that Evans's defense of empiricism* might actually turn students away from more conceptual thinking. As the historian R. D. Anderson* observed in 2001: "On the whole, British students do not need to be warned against the excesses of theory; the problem is rather to arouse an interest in more than the most empirical approach, and it would be a pity if Evans's book was thought to legitimize anti-theoretical attitudes."[3] While many historians would agree with Evans about the dangers of extreme relativism,* and the associated idea that objectivity is impossible to achieve, they were wary in case *In Defence of History* was used as a way of trying to close off conversation with other disciplines.

Schools of Thought

While *In Defence of History* is important, particularly for students, teachers, and some historians, its influence on the intellectual practice of history has declined in the last few years. Many of the ideas within the work can be traced to other historians and were already well established in the mainstream of historical thought. What this book offered instead was a new and outspoken defense of existing practices of history, and it raised important questions about the public role and visibility of historians. This has become a vital topic in light of the popularity of historical programming on British television and the commercial appeal of history publishing, as well as historians' roles in advising on curriculum reform. *In Defence of History* has been followed by a number of books reflecting on how historians communicate their research with a broad audience, and how their scholarship impacts upon broader representations of the past.[4]

The overview given by Evans of the development of the historical profession belongs to a wider fascination with the history of history over the past three decades.[5] Sometimes this had led to attempts to revive the importance of particular historians. For instance, the historian David Cannadine* wrote a very admiring tribute to the popular early twentieth-century British historian G. M. Trevelyan* (although Evans suspected that this nostalgic "patrician" writer would "continue to be neglected in the future").[6] More recently Michael Bentley* has demonstrated "modernist" approaches that revitalized historiography* in Britain in the early twentieth century—drawing attention to shared patterns of thought and stylistic techniques.[7] But it has also led to a greater awareness of the different media through which historical narratives are communicated in the modern world—including theatre, film, TV, and radio—and how these narratives inform cultural memory.[8] As one of the most prominent and decorated historians in Britain, Evans illustrates and comments on the growing presence of historians in public life.

In Current Scholarship

While many of the ideas expressed in the work are not new or at the cutting edge, *In Defence of History* has had a significant impact on the field of history and has been cited in many subsequent works. The book outlines a general defense for history as a discipline against extreme postmodern challenges, rather than for any specific methodology or subject of study. As such, the scope of the work is perhaps too wide-ranging to have inspired the formation of any specific schools. Nonetheless it has been cited in numerous recent discussions of historical method: these include a 2012 article on the use of archives, a 2010 article examining various defenses of historical inquiry, and a 2000 article on history, the Holocaust, and historiography.[9]

The force of Evans's argument against certain aspects of postmodern theory may cause some readers to assume he rejects all postmodern ideas. Keith Jenkins* suggests that while Evans appears to be conciliatory toward some elements of postmodern thinking, this is merely a tactic used to mask his antipathy towards its ideas.[10] Yet Evans, by contrast, insisted on the benefits that could be gained by adopting some of postmodernism's methodological questions, while rejecting its corrosive ideas about the impossibility of reaching truth.[11] To that extent, Evans predicted that postmodernism could be tempered and assimilated as a "legitimate sub specialism." He compared the process to that by which rock and roll started as a form of youth revolt but was co-opted into simply being a musical style, shorn of its radical edge.[12] And in this Evans has been vindicated. Postmodern scholarship has been incorporated into some university departments, just as postmodern ideas have been integrated into the arsenal of historian's approaches.

NOTES

1   John Tosh, *Why History Matters* (Basingstoke: Palgrave Macmillan, 2008); Ludmilla Jordanova, *History in Practice*, 2nd edn (London: Hodder Arnold, 2006).

2   John Tosh, "Shorter Note: In Defence of History," *The English Historical Review* 114 (1999): 805.

3   R. D. Anderson, "Reviews: In Defence of History," *The Scottish Historical Review* 79 (2000): 106.

4   Peter Mandler, *History and National Life* (London: Profile Books, 2002).

5   John Burrow, *A History of Histories: Epics, Chronicles, Romances and Inquiries from Herodotus to the Twentieth Century* (London: Penguin, 2009).

6   David Cannadine, *G.M. Trevelyan: A Life in History* (London: Fontana, 1993); Richard J. Evans, *In Defence of History*, 2nd ed. (London, Granta, 2001), 163,

7   Michael Bentley, *Modernizing England's Pasts: English Historiography in the Age of Modernism 1870–1970* (Cambridge: Cambridge University Press, 2006).

8   Raphael Samuel, *Theatres of Memory: Past and Present in Contemporary Culture*, vol. 1 (London: Verso, 1996).

9   Mary Lindeman, "The Discreet Charm of the Diplomatic Archive," *German History: The Journal of the German History Society*, 29, no. 2 (2011): 283–304; Alexander Lyon Macfie, "On the Defence of (My) History," *Rethinking History: The Journal of Theory and Practice* 14, no. 2 (2010): 209–27; and Michael Dintenfass, "Truth's Other: Ethics, the History of the Holocaust, and Historiographical Theory after the Linguistic Turn," *History and Theory* 39, no. 1 (2000): 1–20.

10 Keith Jenkins, *Why History? Ethics and Postmodernity* (London: Routledge, 1999), 95–114.

11 Evans, *In Defence of History*, 156.

12 Evans, *In Defence of History*, 203.

MODULE 11
IMPACT AND INFLUENCE TODAY

KEY POINTS

- Although *In Defence of History* is still important for under-graduates as an introduction to the methods available to historians, it is not seen as a source of groundbreaking ideas.
- The text contributed to a broader backlash against postmodernism* and the cultural turn* in the early 2000s.
- Evans has been criticized for resorting to polemical attacks—aggressive criticism—and has failed to fully engage with postmodern philosophers.

Position

Richard J. Evans's *In Defence of History* is still used to highlight the controversy concerning the nature of history for university students. This was a central aim of the book and, in this regard, the criticism of the work has enhanced its usefulness. It has further widened the general debate relating to history and brought more students into contact with the key questions of objectivity,* causation, and how history is practiced. Yet these philosophical questions have been bound up in a very polemical exchange of accusations. One reviewer reflected that in the Afterword, in which Evans gives a lengthy rebuttal to his critics, he came across as "petulant and thin-skinned," displaying a "touchy defensiveness" and often resorting to "distasteful" personal attacks.[1]

While the text received great attention at the time of publication and remains a valuable work on the nature of history, less attention has been paid to it in more recent times. Perhaps unsurprisingly, postmodernists like Keith Jenkins* and Alun Munslow* decided to

> ❝ Stimulating debate was one of the book's principal aims; it was never intended to close down discussion (nor would that have been feasible in any case). As those who have attacked the book for failing to confront the major postmodernist thinkers have rightly if somewhat superfluously pointed out, the issues at stake cannot be settled in a couple of hundred pages. So it is important that the debate continues. ❞
>
> Richard J. Evans, Afterword to *In Defence of History*

exclude Evans from their 2004 anthology compiled of 45 different historians, *The Nature of History Reader*.[2] More conventional historians have found the work too broad, and too lacking in originality, to make a decisive contribution. As John Tosh* notes in his 2008 work *Why History Matters*, Evans does not provide any social justification for history or suggest how it could be linked to the wider public.[3] *In Defence of History* is concerned with defending existing ideas of history rather than fully outlining a new practice of history. Yet Evans clearly believes that historians can play a public role in correcting lies told about the Holocaust,* as seen in his role in the libel trial lost by the Holocaust-denier David Irving.*

Interaction

The work continues to ask its readers, both inside and outside academia, to consider the impact of theories that suggest that the reality of the past is secondary or unimportant. For instance, Evans challenges the claim of the Australian scholar Diane Purkiss* that historians should relate the experiences of Jews in Auschwitz* because these stories are so morally "moving"—yet, he writes, "does it really not matter whether or not they are true?"[4] Evans maintains that the scholarly rigor and historical method play an important part in accurately remembering the past and the suffering experienced by individuals.

The "cultural turn" seemed all-powerful in the early 1990s, and introduced many important concepts from French continental philosophy into mainstream historical writing. Yet in the 2000s there have been signs of a backlash against the excesses of histories based purely on discourse—"texts" formed by systems of assumptions and statements—and representation, even among its former champions such as Lynn Hunt.*[5]

Historians in a range of fields sought to find some way of connecting language and discourse back to the lived, social environment (what Evans called "a restoration of a real historical context to language and to thought").[6] This did not necessarily mean turning away from theory. Rather, as distinguished cultural historians like Peter Mandler* suggested, it meant drawing on a wider range of theories and using them in a more critical and pragmatic way. Part of the "problem with cultural history," as Mandler saw it, was that historians had overlooked the "throw" of cultural forms. In other words, they had become too invested in describing discourses and not spent enough time working out why certain discourses were believed, and by which groups, while others were not.[7]

The Continuing Debate

The response from advocates of postmodern philosophy to Evans's work displayed a mixture of intellectual, personal, and political elements. While the point of contention was the intellectual dispute about the concept of objectivity, other criticisms appeared based on individuals' personal resentment toward their treatment in *In Defence of History*. This was due in part to Evans's polemical style. Diane Purkiss described Evans's description of her as a postmodernist* as "hysterical" and accused him of belonging to a "conservative argufying machine."[8]

Although Evans's robust Afterword allows him to deal at length with rival historians, it is clear that he failed to deal sufficiently with the intellectual contribution of thinkers such as Roland Barthes* and Jacques Derrida,* especially noted for their theories relating to language and meaning. The historian R. D. Anderson* regrets that Evans leaves so many "gaps in the picture," especially missing the opportunity to engage constructively with the work of the French social theorist and historian Michel Foucault,* who should have been closest to Evans as a "historian of disease and crime."[9]

Another serious omission from Evans's account is anti-colonial and postcolonial theory. And yet some of the most trenchant attacks on the authority of the historical discipline have come from those scholars who want first to recover the experience of subordinate groups, and second to reframe the way that history is narrated to give equal voice to the colonizers and the colonized. The work of Derrida has been highly influential in this sphere too, with literary critics and historians influenced by deconstruction* describing the existing practice of history as a "white mythology."[10]

For some postcolonial thinkers (that is, thinkers dealing with the various social, historical, and literary legacies of colonialism), this means a concerted effort to "provincialize Europe," in order to find ways of writing history that do not reproduce oppressive Western hierarchies.[11] While *In Defence of History* was effective in fighting off the challenge to notions of objectivity that came from postmodernist relativism*—the idea, roughly, that it is impossible to arrive any objective "truth" through historical research—it does not deal with the methodological challenges that are emerging out of new postcolonial approaches to, and criticisms of, historical research.

NOTES

1   Doug Munro, "*In Defence of History* (review)," *Journal of Social History* 36, no. 1 (2002): 242.

2   Keith Jenkins and Alun Munslow, *The Nature of History Reader* (London: Routledge, 2004).

3   John Tosh, *Why History Matters* (Basingstoke: Palgrave Macmillan, 2008), 18.

4   Richard J. Evans, *In Defence of History*, 2nd ed. (London, Granta, 2001), 242.

5   Lynn Hunt, Victoria Bonnell, and Richard Biernacki, eds., *Beyond the Cultural Turn: New Directions in the Study of Society and Culture* (Berkeley, CA: University of California Press, 1999).

6   Evans, *In Defence of History*, 217.

7   Peter Mandler, "The Problem with Cultural History, or is Playtime Over?," *Cultural and Social History* 1, no. 1 (2004): 94–117.

8   Diane Purkiss, "A Response to Richard J. Evans," *History in Focus*, accessed October 24, 2013, http://www.history.ac.uk/ihr/Focus/ Whatishistory/purkiss1.html. See also Evans, *In Defence of History*, 304, 307.

9   R. D. Anderson, "Review: In Defence of History," *The Scottish Historical Review* 79 (2000): 106.

10   Robert Young, *White Mythologies: Writing, History and the West* (London: Routledge, 1990).

11   Dipesh Chakrabarty, *Provincializing Europe: Postcolonial Thought and Historical Difference* (Princeton, N.J.: Princeton University Press, 2000).

MODULE 12
WHERE NEXT?

KEY POINTS

- *In Defence of History* continues to matter for undergraduate teaching, and retains its importance among the general public as an example of why historians should uphold truthful versions of the past.

- Although it does not present a new mode of studying and writing history, the text has illustrated the diversity in historical practice and theory.

- The impact of *In Defence of History* has been diminishing with the growth of world and global history.

Potential

Since the publication of Richard J. Evans's *In Defence of History* in 1997, the fear that postmodernism* might provide a new paradigm (an overarching intellectual framework inside which solutions to research problems are solved) for historical research has entirely receded—although aspects of postmodern thinking can still be found in American journals like *Representations* and *History & Theory*, where the Dutch philosopher of history Frank Ankersmit* is on the editorial board. There has been a backlash even in literary and philosophical circles against the obsession with describing all social phenomena as an approximation of a literary text. As Evans noted, this analogy does not work, as "most of the time, the majority of people are neither readers nor writers."[1] Beyond this, the 2000s have seen a deeper appreciation of materiality across the humanities—that is, thinkers have been looking at those physical, tactile, embodied forms of knowledge that cannot be reduced to mere discourse.[2]

❝ Historians not only deconstruct the narratives of other historians, they also deconstruct the narratives of the past as well. **❞**

Richard J. Evans, *In Defence of History*

In Defence of History also made clear the public responsibilities of the historian to uphold truth against distortion—a subject with particular relevance and sensitivity in Germany. This theme is addressed by Evans's new book, *The Third Reich in History and Memory* (2015), a collection of his journalism and book reviews, mapping how interpretations of Nazism* have evolved over the past 20 years. Evans shows how the increasing "global turn"* in scholarship—a turn toward the writing of global histories, connecting geographically divided research areas—has led Nazism to be compared to other forms of European empire-building, and, more controversially, how the Holocaust* has been compared to other forms of genocide. Evans weighs the benefits and the dangers of such interpretations, and the collection as a whole testifies to Evans's belief that historians have an ethical duty to describe the past as honestly and responsibly as possible.[3]

Future Directions

In Defence of History describes how the geographical horizon of historians has dramatically expanded since the 1960s. Against skeptics such as G. R. Elton* and Hugh Trevor-Roper,* some historians moved away from prioritizing the history of their own nation or the history of the West to look instead at broader international connections. "Historical scholarship is thus not only more eclectic than ever before," Evans observed approvingly, "it is also becoming gradually less Eurocentric* in its coverage and approach."[4] Yet this very broadening has brought with it fresh problems. For one thing, the growing interest in imperial history has done nothing to reverse the decline in the study of foreign languages in British schools. When Evans published *Cosmopolitan Islanders* in 2009, he wanted to vindicate a tradition of scholarship about Europe that now seemed to be under threat.[5] Second, the big questions about historical method have shifted away from objectivity* and relativism* (central to the postmodernist challenge) to consider how to integrate and do justice to the diverse and often violent experiences of different parts of the globe.[6]

This global dimension has encouraged the pursuit of "big history"—a trend toward considering much longer time-spans and much bigger geographical units than in conventional historical narratives. Evans's own admiration for the influential *Annales* school,* noted for its approach to social history, and disdain for lazy periodization might make him sympathetic to such an approach.[7] The most passionate advocate of this "big history" approach, the Harvard historian David Armitage,* co-authored *The History Manifesto* (2014), aiming to set a new agenda for the discipline. His recommendations include tackling deliberately big data and deliberately big questions, in order to prove the relevance and usefulness of history for government policy.[8] The manifesto has been hugely divisive and subject to extensive and vitriolic criticism.[9] This is a reminder, perhaps, of the difficulties any single scholar faces in trying to define and speak for a historical profession that has become so diverse in its outlook.

Summary

In Defence of History deserves special attention as a passionate, lucid, and entertaining attempt to defend history from postmodern challenges. In the 1980s and 1990s new philosophies of language were applied to the study of history by scholars such as Hayden White,* Frank Ankersmit,* and Keith Jenkins.* Within the work, Evans outlines why history remains a valid discipline. While he recognizes the inescapable role of present-day preoccupations and the force of the historical imagination, Evans insists that the documents that historians use can give them a direct connection to events and people in the past. Evans proposes that some limited form of objectivity is indeed possible, since the nature of the evidence places constrictions on what the historian can say. While good historians will possess "poetry and imagination" in the way they question their sources, documentary evidence allows this to be "disciplined by fact."[10]

While the text is heavily influenced by earlier works of historical theory, especially the Marxist* historian E. H. Carr's* *What Is History?*, its consideration of the "linguistic turn"* and postmodern challenge brings these older arguments up to date for a new generation. However, it is a defense of the mainstream practice of history and, as such, is not a revolutionary work. The text is important because it addresses postmodernism—which questions the purpose, validity, and practices of history—and provides students and teachers with an effective entry point to the debate surrounding the discipline. One of Evans's motivations for writing the book was to indicate that postmodernism can lead to an extreme form of relativism that tolerates fascist and racist ideas, even Holocaust denial. This warning grew directly out of Evans's status as a preeminent social historian* of Germany. The work retains its importance for generating a wide-ranging, sometimes acrimonious, conversation between historians about the purposes and conventions of their profession.

NOTES

1 Richard J. Evans, *In Defence of History*, 2nd ed. (London, Granta: 2001), 186.

2 For an introduction, see Daniel Miller, *Materiality* (Durham, NC: Duke University Press, 2005).

3 Richard J. Evans, *The Third Reich in History and Memory* (New York: Little, Brown, 2015).

4   Evans, *In Defence of History*, 181.

5   Richard J. Evans, *Cosmopolitan Islanders: British Historians and the European Continent* (Cambridge: Cambridge University Press, 2009).

6   Dipesh Chakrabharti, *Provincializing Europe: Postcolonial Thought and Historical Difference* (Princeton: Princeton University Press, 2000).

7   Evans, *In Defence of History*, 156.

8   David Armitage and Jo Guldi, *The History Manifesto* (Cambridge: Cambridge University Press, 2014). Available online: http://historymanifesto.cambridge.org/.

9   Peter Mandler, Deborah Cohen, "The History Manifesto: A Critique," *American Historical Review* 120, no. 2 (2015), 530–42.

10 Evans, *In Defence of History*, 251.

GLOSSARY

GLOSSARY OF TERMS

Annales school: a school of thought named after the French academic journal *Annales d'Histoire Économique et Sociale*. Annales historians sought the creation of history that drew on the aims and methods of different academic disciplines and encompassed the social, psychological, and economic past. Important writers within the Annales include Marc Bloch, Lucien Febvre, and Ferdinand Braudel.

Anti-Semitism: hostility or prejudice towards Jewish people.

Auschwitz: a concentration and extermination camp in Nazi-occupied Poland that was a key site for the mass murder of millions of European Jews.

Cold War (1947–91): a period of military and ideological tension between the capitalist United States and the communist Soviet Union between the end of World War II and 1991. While the two blocs never engaged in direct military conflict, they engaged in covert and proxy wars and espionage against one another.

Cultural turn: refers to the vogue for cultural historical approaches in the 1980s and early 1990s. The cultural turn was inspired in part by bringing history into closer relationship with neighboring disciplines like literary criticism, art history, and social anthropology.

Deconstruction: a movement in literary theory that began in the 1960s and questions the links between meaning and language. The French philosopher Jacques Derrida asserted that texts are inexhaustible in their possible and constantly shifting meanings.

Determinism: among historians "determinism" refers to the belief that certain developments had to occur in a particular way. Determinists discount the role of chance and instead emphasize that certain historical trends and events were necessary and inevitable.

Empiricism: a theory of knowledge that believes that the past, and its truth, can be obtained from a close examination of primary sources and evidence.

Eurocentric: a focus on European assumptions, concerns, history, and culture; historical analysis of international events that primarily considers the implications for Europe.

Feminism: a political movement that seeks to understand and overturn the enduring forms of inequality between the sexes by securing equal political, social, economic, and cultural rights for women.

Global turn: refers to the growing trends towards writing global, trans-national, and international "connective" histories in the 1990s and 2000s.

Great Depression: a global economic downturn that began in the United States following a stock-market crash in 1929.

Historikerstreit: a German term that can be translated as "the historians' quarrel." It arose in West Germany in the 1980s when several conservative historians, including Michael Stürmer and Ernst Nolte, wanted to remove the "guilt" felt by many Germans, and to revise the unique place of the Holocaust in history.

Historiography: the study of historical writing or the study of the evolution of a historical debate over time.

History Workshop: a movement founded in the 1960s by British historian Raphael Samuel. The movement favored "history from below," told from the perspective of ordinary people instead of elites.

Holocaust: the systematic, state-organized deportation and mass extermination of Jews by Nazi Germany during World War II. Some scholars argue that the mass extermination and persecution of other groups, such as socialists, homosexuals, Romani, and those with mental illnesses, should also be included in the definition.

Linguistic turn: a development in a wide number of disciplines that began to focus on the importance of language and philosophies relating to language. The "linguistic turn" was linked to poststructuralist ideas and, in particular, the work of Jacques Derrida.

Marxism: a term used to describe a broad range of approaches in a variety of different fields including history, sociology, economics, and politics. It is based upon the ideas of Karl Marx in the mid-nineteenth century. While there are various strands to Marxist thought, one of its key tenets is the belief in the materialistic development of history, class structures, and the dialectic nature of societal forces. English Marxist historians in the mid-twentieth century include Eric Hobsbawm, Christopher Hill, and E. P. Thompson.

Material turn: a school of thought that emerged in the 1990s and 2000s. It was inspired by scholars in archaeology, art history, and anthropology. Its practitioners wanted to encourage scholars to think more about the non-discursive properties of objects and things.

Meta-narrative: a writing methodology that describe narratives that aim to give a total or comprehensive account of historical change, and suggest that history is necessarily moving in a certain progressive direction. Postmodernists have claimed that meta-narratives are oppressive or no longer relevant.

Nazi Germany: refers to the period of rule in Germany by the extremely right-wing Nationalist Socialist German Workers' (Nazi) Party led by Adolf Hitler between 1933 and 1945. Nazism is the name for the political movement and ideology created by the Nazi Party.

New Left: a term used in Britain and America to describe a movement of the late 1960s and 1970s that sought to implement wide-ranging social reforms, but rejected the approach of the traditional left-wing and Marxist parties.

Objectivity: the belief that there are real phenomena that exist, which can be judged or observed, and are independent of emotional or personal prejudices.

Postmodernism: a wide-ranging term applied to many disciplines to describe a set of beliefs that are considered to have emerged in the early twentieth century. It is usually said to include a belief that reality is a construct of the human mind. It involves an intrinsic rejection of universal laws, values, or concepts. In history, the idea of postmodernism places an emphasis on the difficulty, or impossibility, of representing the past in the present, the subjective nature of historical research, and the role of language in the historical work.

Relativism: a term given to a family of concepts that suggests there is no absolute or universal truth, knowledge, or morality, and that such ideas are intrinsically related to culture, historical circumstances, or society.

Social history: a branch of history that seeks to investigate not just the political elite but all the groups within a past society; social historians have typically been drawn to the study of different social classes, living conditions, and family relations. Influenced often by Marxism, social history saw dramatic expansion in the 1960s and 1970s, although its appeal waned in the 1980s and 1990s.

Soviet Union (or USSR): a kind of "super state" that existed from 1922 to 1991, centered primarily on Russia and its neighbors in Eastern Europe and the northern half of Asia. It was the communist pole of the Cold War, with the United States as its main "rival."

Teleology: the belief that things move inevitably towards a certain goal or end; in the case of history, teleological thinking implies that there is a purpose and a general direction driving social development.

Third Reich: the name for the regime created by Adolf Hitler and the Nazi Party in Germany between 1933 and their defeat in World War II in 1945. Intended to last a thousand years, like the first Holy Roman Empire, it lasted merely twelve.

Wilhelmine Germany: refers to Imperial Germany between 1871 and 1918, and in particular between 1888 and 1918, when it was ruled by Kasier Wilhelm II.

World War I (1914–18): a mass conflict that began between the empires of Europe, but expanded to bring in the United States and much of the colonial world, and ended with the defeat of Germany and its allies.

World War II (1939–45): a global conflict that ended with the Allies (Britain, France, the United States, and the Soviet Union) defeating the Axis powers (Nazi Germany, Fascist Italy, and Imperial Japan).

PEOPLE MENTIONED IN THE TEXT

David Abraham is a professor of law at the University of Miami. As a young historian in Princeton he received considerable attention for his book *The Collapse of the Weimar Republic* in 1981. The book was subject to hostile criticism for the way it manipulated sources, overlooked counter-evidence and took a partisan line to claim that big business helped bring the Nazis to power.

R. D. Anderson is a professor of history at Edinburgh University, and has worked on educational systems in France and Scotland.

Joyce Appleby (b. 1929) is an American historian who specializes in historiography and the political and economic thought of the early American Republic.

Frank R. Ankersmit (b. 1945) is a Dutch philosopher of history. He is currently professor of intellectual history and historical theory at the University of Groningen, the Netherlands.

David Armitage (b. 1965) is a historian of intellectual and international history at Harvard University. He is the joint author (with Jo Guldi) of the controversial 2014 *History Manifesto*.

Roland Barthes (1915–80) was a French literary theorist, linguist, and philosopher. He contributed to many different theories including structuralism and post-structuralism.

Catherine Belsey (b. 1940) is a literary critic and visiting professor at the University of Derby, who has been a constant champion of innovative and postmodern theoretical approaches.

Michael Bentley (b. 1948) is a historian of Victorian British politics and twentieth-century intellectual culture.

David Cannadine (b. 1950) is a British historian who specializes in the history of nineteenth- and twentieth-century Britain, writing classic books on aristocracy, empire, and monarchy. He is also a major advisor on the teaching of history in British schools.

Jane Caplan is a historian whose main interest lies in Nazi Germany. She has held many academic positions in both America and Britain.

E. H. Carr (1892–1982) was a British Marxist historian who wrote a classic history of interwar diplomacy and the history of the Soviet Union. His 1961 book *What Is History?* was a huge influence on Richard J. Evans.

Stefan Collini (b. 1947) is an English literary critic and professor of intellectual history at Cambridge. He specializes in British nineteenth- and twentieth-century high culture.

Robert Darnton (b. 1939) is an American historian who specializes in eighteenth-century France and the history of the book. His classic study *The Great Cat Massacre* (1984) was discussed by Richard J. Evans as an example of how some postmodern ideas could inform cultural history.

Paul de Man (1919–83) was a Belgian-born literary theorist who settled in America and taught at Harvard. A key theorist of deconstruction, in the 1980s it was revealed that de Man had written a number of anti-Semitic articles for a collaborationist newspaper in Belgium during World War II. The resulting controversy saw Derrida and his critics trade accusations about the relationship between de Man's philosophical views and political conduct.

Jacques Derrida (1930–2004) was an Algerian-born French philosopher, who was noted for his development of deconstruction and poststructuralism. One of Derrida's most quoted (and misquoted) phrases was *"il n'y a pas d'hors-texte"*—in other words, there is nothing outside or beyond the text.

Anthony Easthope (1939–99) was a professor in English studies at Manchester Metropolitan University, known for his iconoclastic reviews of established critics, as well as his openness to continental philosophy and intellectual innovation.

G. R. Elton (1921–94) was a German-born British historian who specialized in the Tudor period, believing that the 1530s saw the development of centralized administration and a "revolution in government." He was fiercely critical of Marxist historians and departures from political or national history.

Niall Ferguson (b. 1964) is a British historian, particularly known for his works on financial, international, and imperial history. He is also known for his own media career and role as an advisor to the British government over history teaching in schools.

Fritz Fischer (1908–99) was an influential German historian who is most famous for his groundbreaking work on World War I.

Michel Foucault (1926–84) was a French philosopher who wrote seminal work on epistemology, discourse, sexuality, and the discipline exercised by social institutions. Foucault is undoubtedly one of the most important thinkers since World War II—and his omission from Richard J. Evans's discussion is striking.

Thomas L. Haskell (b. 1939) is an American historian who has a particular interest in American history. He is Samuel G. McCann Professor Emeritus of History at Rice University, Houston.

Christopher Hill (1912–2003) was a British Marxist historian who focused mainly on seventeenth-century Britain and studied the radical groups of democrats and dissenters who flourished during the English Civil War.

Gertrude Himmelfarb (b. 1922) is an American historian who has written on the intellectual culture of Victorian Britain and calls for a return to traditional and conservative approaches to history.

Lynn Hunt (b. 1945) is an American historian, known for her works on the French Revolution and the theory of history. She was one of the most prominent champions of the cultural turn in the early 1990s.

David Irving (b. 1938) is a British author who has gained notoriety for his works on World War II and Nazi Germany. One of the leaders of Holocaust "revisionism," Irving was arrested and imprisoned in 2006 in Austria, where Holocaust denial is illegal.

Keith Jenkins (b. 1943) is a British postmodern historian and philosopher of history. Jenkins responds to Richard J. Evans in *Why History? Ethics and Postmodernity*.

Ludmilla Jordanova (b. 1949) is a British historian who is currently a professor at the University of Durham. She has produced works on gender and medicine in history, as well as a work on the nature of historical practice and the uses of visual culture.

Deborah Lipstadt (b. 1947) is an American historian noted for her works on the Holocaust. She is the Dorot Professor of Modern Jewish and Holocaust Studies at Emory University, Atlanta.

Peter Mandler (b. 1958) is professor of history at Cambridge and an expert on British nineteenth- and twentieth-century cultural history. He has written extensively on the development of heritage in modern Britain, as well as the relationship between history and the social sciences.

Doug Munro is an adjunct professor at the University of Queensland in New Zealand who works on historical biography and the twentieth-century Pacific.

Alun Munslow (b. 1947) is professor of history at Staffordshire University, known as a champion of postmodern and deconstructionist approaches.

Peter Novick (1934–2012) is an American historian who is particularly known for his works on the theory of history.

Diane Purkiss (b. 1961) is an Australian historian who has written about gender and literature, witchcraft, and the English Civil War.

Leopold von Ranke (1795–1886) was a German historian at the University of Berlin who laid the foundations of source-based criticism and is hence regarded as the father of the discipline. He worked extensively on the history of religion and diplomacy in early modern Europe.

Joan Wallach Scott (b. 1941) is an American historian based at Princeton. She has published widely on French social and cultural history, and is one of the most important thinkers on gender and feminist history.

Joseph Stalin (1878–1953) was dictator of the Soviet Union, ruling as General Secretary of the Communist Party from 1928 (when he eliminated his rivals) through to his death in 1953. Stalin's policies included forced collectivization of agriculture and forced industrialization—often at terrible human cost—and terrorization and purges of his enemies.

Lawrence Stone (1919–99) was a British historian of the early modern period who taught at Oxford and Princeton. Richard J. Evans cites his notorious clash with Hugh Trevor-Roper over an article in which Stone had claimed that there was a decline in the economic power of the aristocracy on the eve of the English Civil War—an argument that Trevor-Roper demolished by exposing Stone's misuse and misreading of the sources.

Keith Thomas (b. 1933) is a British historian who was professor of modern history at Oxford from 1986 to 2000. A pioneer in borrowing methods from anthropology, Thomas has written on magic, superstition, religion, and ideas about nature in early modern Britain.

Thucydides (460–395 B.C.E.) was one of the greatest Greek historians, author of a devastating history of the Peloponnesian War between Athens and Sparta.

John Tosh is a British historian who is currently professor of history at Roehampton University. He has gained note for his works on masculinity in history and the nature of history.

G. M. Trevelyan (1876–1962) was a British historian noted for his works on seventeenth- to nineteenth-century British politics and his espousal of Whig/Liberal ideas. He was also a pioneer in the field of social history, even if Richard J. Evans was dismissive of his literary and patrician approach to the subject.

Hugh Trevor-Roper (1914–2003) was Regius Professor of Modern History at Oxford. A specialist in early modern Britain and Europe, he was also an early writer on the Third Reich, but his reputation became tarnished through his decision to authenticate bogus Hitler diaries in the 1980s.

Hayden V. White (b. 1928) is an American historian who has provided many works of historical theory linked to literary criticism. He argues for all historical writing involving a form of narrative "emplotment."

Natalie Zemon-Davis (b. 1928) is a Canadian-born historian of early modern Europe, famed for her groundbreaking work on women's history, the boundaries between history and anthropology, and the place of fiction and story-telling in the archives.

WORKS CITED

WORKS CITED

Anderson, R. D. "Reviews: In Defence of History." *Scottish Historical Review* 79 (2000): 105–6.

Ankersmit, F.R. *Historical Representation*. Stanford, CA: Stanford University Press, 2002.

― ― ―. *Narrative Logic: A Semantic Analysis of the Historian's Language*. The Hague: Martinus Nijhoff, 1983.

― ― ―. *Sublime Historical Experience*. Stanford, CA: Stanford University Press, 2005.

Appleby, Joyce Oldham. "Does It Really Need Defending?" *The Times Literary Supplement*, October 25, 1997.

Appleby, Joyce Oldham, Margaret C. Jacob, and Lynn Hunt. *Telling the Truth about History*. New York and London: Norton, 1994.

Armitage, David, and Jo Guldi. *The History Manifesto*. Cambridge: Cambridge University Press, 2014. Available online: http://historymanifesto.cambridge.org/.

Barthes, Roland. *Image, Music, Text*. Translated by Stephen Heath. London: Flamingo, 1984.

Belsey, Catherine. "In Defence of History," *European Journal of English Studies* 3, no. 1 (1999): 106–13.

Bentley, Michael. *Modernizing England's Pasts: English Historiography in the Age of Modernism 1870–1970*. Cambridge: Cambridge University Press, 2006.

Burrow, John. *A History of Histories: Epics, Chronicles, Romances and Inquiries from Herodotus to the Twentieth Century*. London: Penguin, 2009.

Cannadine, David. *G.M. Trevelyan: A Life in History*. London: Fontana, 1993.

― ― ―. *What Is History Now?* Basingstoke: Palgrave Macmillan, 2002.

Caplan, Jane. *Government without Administration: State and Civil Service in Weimar and Nazi Germany*. Oxford: Clarendon Press, 1989.

― ― ―. "Postmodernism, Poststructuralism, and Deconstruction: Notes for Historians." *Central European History* 22, nos 3–4 (1989): 260–78.

Carr, E. H. *What Is History?* Introduced by Richard J. Evans. Fortieth anniversary ed. Basingstoke: Palgrave, 2001.

Carr, E. H., and R. W. Davies. *A History of Soviet Russia*. London: Macmillan, 1978.

Chakrabarty, Dipesh. *Provincializing Europe: Postcolonial Thought and Historical Difference*. Princeton, N.J.: Princeton University Press, 2000.

Collini, Stefan. "The Truth Vandals," *Guardian*, December 18, 1997.

Derrida, Jacques. *Of Grammatology*. Translated by Gayatri Chakravorty Spivak. Baltimore and London: Johns Hopkins University Press, 1997.

— — —. *Writing and Difference*. Translated by Alan Bass. London: Routledge, 2001.

Dintenfass, Michael. "Truth's Other: Ethics, the History of the Holocaust, and Historiographical Theory after the Linguistic Turn." *History and Theory* 39, no. 1 (2000): 1–20.

Easthope, Anthony. *Textual Practice, 12, no. 3* (1998): 563–6.

Elton, G. R. *The Practice of History*. Sydney: Methuen, 1967.

Evans, Richard J. *The Coming of the Third Reich*. London: Allen Lane, 2003.

— — —. *Cosmopolitan Islanders: British Historians and the European Continent*. Cambridge: Cambridge University Press, 2009.

— — —. *Death in Hamburg: Society and Politics in the Cholera Years, 1830– 1910*. Oxford: Clarendon Press, 1987.

— — —. *In Defence of History*. 2nd ed. London: Granta, 2001.

— — —. *The Feminist Movement in Germany 1894–1933*. London: Sage Publications, 1976.

— — —. *In Hitler's Shadow: West German Historians and the Attempt to Escape from the Nazi Past*. New York: Pantheon Books, 1989.

— — —. "The New Nationalism and the Old History: Perspectives on the West German *Historikerstreit*." *Journal of Modern History* 59, no. 4 (1987): 761–97.

— — —. "Review: *The Annales School: An Intellectual History* by André Burguière." *London Review of Books* 31, no. 23 (December 3, 2009): 12–14.

— — —. *Rituals of Retribution: Capital Punishment in Germany 1600–1987*. Oxford: Oxford University Press, 1996.

— — —. *Society and Politics in Wilhelmine Germany*. London: Croom Helm, 1978.

— — —. *Tales from the German Underworld: Crime and Punishment in the Nineteenth Century*. New Haven, CT, and London: Yale University Press, 1998.

— — —. *Telling Lies about Hitler: The Holocaust, History and the David Irving Trial*. London: Verso, 2002.

— — —. *The Third Reich in Power, 1933–1939*. London: Allen Lane, 2005.

— — —. *The Third Reich at War, 1939–1945*. London: Allen Lane, 2008.

Ferguson, Niall. "History Is Dead, Long Live History!" *Sunday Times*, September 21, 1997.

— — —. *The War of the World: History's Age of Hatred*. London: Allen Lane, 2006.

Fischer, Fritz. *War of Illusions: German Policies from 1911 to 1914*. Translated by Marian Jackson. London: Chatto & Windus, 1975.

Foucault, Michel. *The Archaeology of Knowledge*. Translated by Alan Sheridan. London: Tavistock Publications, 1972.

— — —. *The History of Sexuality*. Translated by Robert Hurley. London: Allen Lane, 1979.

— — —. *The Order of Things: An Archaeology of the Human Sciences*. London: Routledge, 2001.

Hamerow, Theodor S. "Guilt, Redemption and Writing German History." *American Historical Review* 88, February (1983): 53–72.

Haskell, Thomas L. *Objectivity Is Not Neutrality: Explanatory Schemes in History*. Baltimore and London: Johns Hopkins University Press, 1998.

Hill, Christopher. *The Century of Revolution, 1603–1714*. London: Routledge, 2002.

— — —. *Puritanism and Revolution: Studies in Interpretation of the English Revolution of the Seventeenth Century*. Harmondsworth: Penguin, 1986.

Hunt, Lynn. "Does History Need Defending?" *History Workshop Journal* 46, December (1998): 241–9.

Hunt, Lynn, Bonnell, Victoria, and Biernacki, Richard, eds. *Beyond the Cultural Turn: New Directions in the Study of Society and Culture*. Berkeley: University of California Press, 1999.

Jenkins, Keith. *Re-Thinking History*. With a New Preface and Conversation with the Author by Alun Munslow. London: Routledge, 2003.

— — —. *On "What Is History?" From Carr and Elton to Rorty and White*. London: Routledge, 1995.

— — —. *Why History? Ethics and Postmodernity*. London: Routledge, 1999.

Jenkins, Keith, and Alun Munslow. *The Nature of History Reader*. London: Routledge, 2004.

Jordanova, Ludmilla. *History in Practice*. 2nd ed. London: Hodder Arnold, 2006.

Joyce, Patrick. *The Social in Question: New Bearings in History and the Social Sciences*. London: Routledge, 2002.

Kenyon, J.P. *The History Men: The Historical Profession in England since the Renaissance*. 2nd ed. London: Weidenfeld & Nicolson, 1993.

Lindeman, Mary. "The Discreet Charm of the Diplomatic Archive." *German History: The Journal of the German History Society* 29, no. 2 (1984): 283–304.

Lipstadt, Deborah E. *Denying the Holocaust: The Growing Assault on Truth and Memory*. London: Penguin, 1994.

———. *History on Trial: My Day in Court with David Irving*. New York: HarperPerennial, 2006.

Macfie, Alexander Lyon. "On the Defence of (My) History." *Rethinking History: The Journal of Theory and Practice* 14, no. 2 (2010): 209–27.

Mandler, Peter. *History and National Life*. London: Profile Books, 2002.

———. "The Problem with Cultural History, or is Playtime Over?" *Cultural and Social History* 1, no. 1 (2004): 94–117.

Mandler, Peter, and Deborah Cohen. "The History Manifesto: A Critique."

American Historical Review 120, no. 2 (2015): 530–42.

Marx, Karl, and Friedrich Engels. *The Communist Manifesto*. Edited and introduced by Jeffrey C. Isaac. New Haven, CT: Yale University Press, 2012.

Marx, Karl, and Hugo Gellert. *Karl Marx' 'Capital'*. Baarle-Nassau: SoMa, 1981.

Miller, Daniel, ed. *Materiality*. Durham, NC: Duke University Press, 2005.

Munro, Doug. "*In Defence of History* (Review)." *Journal of Social History* 36, no. 1 (2002): 242–4.

Munslow, Alun. *Deconstructing History*. 2nd ed. London: Routledge, 2006.

———. *Narrative and History*. Basingstoke: Palgrave Macmillan, 2007.

Novick, Peter. *The Holocaust and Collective Memory: The American Experience*. London: Bloomsbury, 2000.

———. *That Noble Dream: The "Objectivity Question" and the American Historical Profession*. Cambridge: Cambridge University Press, 1988.

Parkin, Frank. *Marxism and Class Theory: A Bourgeois Critique*. London: Tavistock Publications, 1981, c. 1979.

Purdue, A. W. "Book of the Week: Cosmopolitan Islanders." *Times Higher Education*, July 9, 2009. Accessed October 24, 2013. http://www.timeshighereducation.co.uk/407279.article.

Purkiss, Diane. "A Response to Richard J. Evans." *History in Focus*. Accessed October 24, 2013. http://www.history.ac.uk/ihr/Focus/Whatishistory/purkiss1.html.

— — —. *The Witch in History: Early Modern and Twentieth-Century Representations*. London: Routledge, 1996.

Ranke, Leopold von. *History of the Latin and Teutonic Nations, 1494 to 1514*. Translated by G.R. Dennis. Introduction by E. Armstrong. London: Bell, 1915.

"Richard J. Evans—In Defence of History." *Kirkus Reviews*, November 1, 1998.

Samuel, Raphael. *History Workshop: A Collectanea 1967–1991*. London: History Workshop, 1991.

— — —. *Theatres of Memory: Past and Present in Contemporary Culture*, vol. 1. London: Verso, 1996.

Samuel, Raphael, Jennie Kitteringham, and David M. Morgan. *Village Life and Labour*. Edited by Raphael Samuel. London: Routledge & Kegan Paul, 1975.

Snowman, Daniel. "Daniel Snowman Meets the Historian of Germany, Defender of History and Expert Witness in the Irving Trial." *History Today* 54 (January 2004): 45–7.

Thomas, Keith. *Religion and the Decline of Magic: Studies in Popular Beliefs in Sixteenth- and Seventeenth-Century England*. Harmondsworth: Penguin, 1978.

Tosh, John. "Shorter Note: In Defence of History." *The English Historical Review* 114 (1999): 805–6.

Tosh, John. *Why History Matters*. Basingstoke: Palgrave Macmillan, 2008.

Tosh, John, and Sean Lang. *The Pursuit of History: Aims, Methods and New Directions in the Study of Modern History*. 4th ed. Harlow: Longman, 2006.

Trevelyan, G.M.. *British History in the Nineteenth Century (1782–1939)*. [S.l.]: [s.n.], 1947.

— — —. *The English Revolution, 1688–1689*. [S.l.]: [s.n.], 1956.

Trevor-Roper, H.R. *The Last Days of Hitler*. 7th ed. London: Papermac, 1995.

White, Hayden. *The Content of Form: Narrative Discourse and Historical Representation*. Baltimore and London: Johns Hopkins University Press, 1987.

———. *Metahistory: The Historical Imagination in Nineteenth-Century Europe*. Baltimore and London: Johns Hopkins University Press, 1975.

———. *Tropics of Discourse: Essays in Cultural Criticism*. Baltimore and London: Johns Hopkins University Press, 1978.

Young, Robert, *White Mythologies: Writing, History and the West*. London: Routledge, 1990.

THE MACAT LIBRARY
BY DISCIPLINE

AFRICANA STUDIES

Chinua Achebe's *An Image of Africa: Racism in Conrad's Heart of Darkness*
W. E. B. Du Bois's *The Souls of Black Folk*
Zora Neale Huston's *Characteristics of Negro Expression*
Martin Luther King Jr's *Why We Can't Wait*
Toni Morrison's *Playing in the Dark: Whiteness in the American Literary Imagination*

ANTHROPOLOGY

Arjun Appadurai's *Modernity at Large: Cultural Dimensions of Globalisation*
Philippe Ariès's *Centuries of Childhood*
Franz Boas's *Race, Language and Culture*
Kim Chan & Renée Mauborgne's *Blue Ocean Strategy*
Jared Diamond's *Guns, Germs & Steel: the Fate of Human Societies*
Jared Diamond's *Collapse: How Societies Choose to Fail or Survive*
E. E. Evans-Pritchard's *Witchcraft, Oracles and Magic Among the Azande*
James Ferguson's *The Anti-Politics Machine*
Clifford Geertz's *The Interpretation of Cultures*
David Graeber's *Debt: the First 5000 Years*
Karen Ho's *Liquidated: An Ethnography of Wall Street*
Geert Hofstede's *Culture's Consequences: Comparing Values, Behaviors, Institutes and Organizations across Nations*
Claude Lévi-Strauss's *Structural Anthropology*
Jay Macleod's *Ain't No Makin' It: Aspirations and Attainment in a Low-Income Neighborhood*
Saba Mahmood's *The Politics of Piety: The Islamic Revival and the Feminist Subject*
Marcel Mauss's *The Gift*

BUSINESS

Jean Lave & Etienne Wenger's *Situated Learning*
Theodore Levitt's *Marketing Myopia*
Burton G. Malkiel's *A Random Walk Down Wall Street*
Douglas McGregor's *The Human Side of Enterprise*
Michael Porter's *Competitive Strategy: Creating and Sustaining Superior Performance*
John Kotter's *Leading Change*
C. K. Prahalad & Gary Hamel's *The Core Competence of the Corporation*

CRIMINOLOGY

Michelle Alexander's *The New Jim Crow: Mass Incarceration in the Age of Colorblindness*
Michael R. Gottfredson & Travis Hirschi's *A General Theory of Crime*
Richard Herrnstein & Charles A. Murray's *The Bell Curve: Intelligence and Class Structure in American Life*
Elizabeth Loftus's *Eyewitness Testimony*
Jay Macleod's *Ain't No Makin' It: Aspirations and Attainment in a Low-Income Neighborhood*
Philip Zimbardo's *The Lucifer Effect*

ECONOMICS

Janet Abu-Lughod's *Before European Hegemony*
Ha-Joon Chang's *Kicking Away the Ladder*
David Brion Davis's *The Problem of Slavery in the Age of Revolution*
Milton Friedman's *The Role of Monetary Policy*
Milton Friedman's *Capitalism and Freedom*
David Graeber's *Debt: the First 5000 Years*
Friedrich Hayek's *The Road to Serfdom*
Karen Ho's *Liquidated: An Ethnography of Wall Street*

John Maynard Keynes's *The General Theory of Employment, Interest and Money*
Charles P. Kindleberger's *Manias, Panics and Crashes*
Robert Lucas's *Why Doesn't Capital Flow from Rich to Poor Countries?*
Burton G. Malkiel's *A Random Walk Down Wall Street*
Thomas Robert Malthus's *An Essay on the Principle of Population*
Karl Marx's *Capital*
Thomas Piketty's *Capital in the Twenty-First Century*
Amartya Sen's *Development as Freedom*
Adam Smith's *The Wealth of Nations*
Nassim Nicholas Taleb's *The Black Swan: The Impact of the Highly Improbable*
Amos Tversky's & Daniel Kahneman's *Judgment under Uncertainty: Heuristics and Biases*
Mahbub Ul Haq's *Reflections on Human Development*
Max Weber's *The Protestant Ethic and the Spirit of Capitalism*

FEMINISM AND GENDER STUDIES

Judith Butler's *Gender Trouble*
Simone De Beauvoir's *The Second Sex*
Michel Foucault's *History of Sexuality*
Betty Friedan's *The Feminine Mystique*
Saba Mahmood's *The Politics of Piety: The Islamic Revival and the Feminist Subject*
Joan Wallach Scott's *Gender and the Politics of History*
Mary Wollstonecraft's *A Vindication of the Rights of Woman*
Virginia Woolf's *A Room of One's Own*

GEOGRAPHY

The Brundtland Report's *Our Common Future*
Rachel Carson's *Silent Spring*
Charles Darwin's *On the Origin of Species*
James Ferguson's *The Anti-Politics Machine*
Jane Jacobs's *The Death and Life of Great American Cities*
James Lovelock's *Gaia: A New Look at Life on Earth*
Amartya Sen's *Development as Freedom*
Mathis Wackernagel & William Rees's *Our Ecological Footprint*

HISTORY

Janet Abu-Lughod's *Before European Hegemony*
Benedict Anderson's *Imagined Communities*
Bernard Bailyn's *The Ideological Origins of the American Revolution*
Hanna Batatu's *The Old Social Classes And The Revolutionary Movements Of Iraq*
Christopher Browning's *Ordinary Men: Reserve Police Batallion 101 and the Final Solution in Poland*
Edmund Burke's *Reflections on the Revolution in France*
William Cronon's *Nature's Metropolis: Chicago And The Great West*
Alfred W. Crosby's *The Columbian Exchange*
Hamid Dabashi's *Iran: A People Interrupted*
David Brion Davis's *The Problem of Slavery in the Age of Revolution*
Nathalie Zemon Davis's *The Return of Martin Guerre*
Jared Diamond's *Guns, Germs & Steel: the Fate of Human Societies*
Frank Dikotter's *Mao's Great Famine*
John W Dower's *War Without Mercy: Race And Power In The Pacific War*
W. E. B. Du Bois's *The Souls of Black Folk*
Richard J. Evans's *In Defence of History*
Lucien Febvre's *The Problem of Unbelief in the 16th Century*
Sheila Fitzpatrick's *Everyday Stalinism*

The Macat Library By Discipline

Eric Foner's *Reconstruction: America's Unfinished Revolution, 1863-1877*
Michel Foucault's *Discipline and Punish*
Michel Foucault's *History of Sexuality*
Francis Fukuyama's *The End of History and the Last Man*
John Lewis Gaddis's *We Now Know: Rethinking Cold War History*
Ernest Gellner's *Nations and Nationalism*
Eugene Genovese's *Roll, Jordan, Roll: The World the Slaves Made*
Carlo Ginzburg's *The Night Battles*
Daniel Goldhagen's *Hitler's Willing Executioners*
Jack Goldstone's *Revolution and Rebellion in the Early Modern World*
Antonio Gramsci's *The Prison Notebooks*
Alexander Hamilton, John Jay & James Madison's *The Federalist Papers*
Christopher Hill's *The World Turned Upside Down*
Carole Hillenbrand's *The Crusades: Islamic Perspectives*
Thomas Hobbes's *Leviathan*
Eric Hobsbawm's *The Age Of Revolution*
John A. Hobson's *Imperialism: A Study*
Albert Hourani's *History of the Arab Peoples*
Samuel P. Huntington's *The Clash of Civilizations and the Remaking of World Order*
C. L. R. James's *The Black Jacobins*
Tony Judt's *Postwar: A History of Europe Since 1945*
Ernst Kantorowicz's *The King's Two Bodies: A Study in Medieval Political Theology*
Paul Kennedy's *The Rise and Fall of the Great Powers*
Ian Kershaw's *The "Hitler Myth": Image and Reality in the Third Reich*
John Maynard Keynes's *The General Theory of Employment, Interest and Money*
Charles P. Kindleberger's *Manias, Panics and Crashes*
Martin Luther King Jr's *Why We Can't Wait*
Henry Kissinger's *World Order: Reflections on the Character of Nations and the Course of History*
Thomas Kuhn's *The Structure of Scientific Revolutions*
Georges Lefebvre's *The Coming of the French Revolution*
John Locke's *Two Treatises of Government*
Niccolò Machiavelli's *The Prince*
Thomas Robert Malthus's *An Essay on the Principle of Population*
Mahmood Mamdani's *Citizen and Subject: Contemporary Africa And The Legacy Of Late Colonialism*
Karl Marx's *Capital*
Stanley Milgram's *Obedience to Authority*
John Stuart Mill's *On Liberty*
Thomas Paine's *Common Sense*
Thomas Paine's *Rights of Man*
Geoffrey Parker's *Global Crisis: War, Climate Change and Catastrophe in the Seventeenth Century*
Jonathan Riley-Smith's *The First Crusade and the Idea of Crusading*
Jean-Jacques Rousseau's *The Social Contract*
Joan Wallach Scott's *Gender and the Politics of History*
Theda Skocpol's *States and Social Revolutions*
Adam Smith's *The Wealth of Nations*
Timothy Snyder's *Bloodlands: Europe Between Hitler and Stalin*
Sun Tzu's *The Art of War*
Keith Thomas's *Religion and the Decline of Magic*
Thucydides's *The History of the Peloponnesian War*
Frederick Jackson Turner's *The Significance of the Frontier in American History*
Odd Arne Westad's *The Global Cold War: Third World Interventions And The Making Of Our Times*

LITERATURE

Chinua Achebe's *An Image of Africa: Racism in Conrad's Heart of Darkness*
Roland Barthes's *Mythologies*
Homi K. Bhabha's *The Location of Culture*
Judith Butler's *Gender Trouble*
Simone De Beauvoir's *The Second Sex*
Ferdinand De Saussure's *Course in General Linguistics*
T. S. Eliot's *The Sacred Wood: Essays on Poetry and Criticism*
Zora Neale Huston's *Characteristics of Negro Expression*
Toni Morrison's *Playing in the Dark: Whiteness in the American Literary Imagination*
Edward Said's *Orientalism*
Gayatri Chakravorty Spivak's *Can the Subaltern Speak?*
Mary Wollstonecraft's *A Vindication of the Rights of Women*
Virginia Woolf's *A Room of One's Own*

PHILOSOPHY

Elizabeth Anscombe's *Modern Moral Philosophy*
Hannah Arendt's *The Human Condition*
Aristotle's *Metaphysics*
Aristotle's *Nicomachean Ethics*
Edmund Gettier's *Is Justified True Belief Knowledge?*
Georg Wilhelm Friedrich Hegel's *Phenomenology of Spirit*
David Hume's *Dialogues Concerning Natural Religion*
David Hume's *The Enquiry for Human Understanding*
Immanuel Kant's *Religion within the Boundaries of Mere Reason*
Immanuel Kant's *Critique of Pure Reason*
Søren Kierkegaard's *The Sickness Unto Death*
Søren Kierkegaard's *Fear and Trembling*
C. S. Lewis's *The Abolition of Man*
Alasdair MacIntyre's *After Virtue*
Marcus Aurelius's *Meditations*
Friedrich Nietzsche's *On the Genealogy of Morality*
Friedrich Nietzsche's *Beyond Good and Evil*
Plato's *Republic*
Plato's *Symposium*
Jean-Jacques Rousseau's *The Social Contract*
Gilbert Ryle's *The Concept of Mind*
Baruch Spinoza's *Ethics*
Sun Tzu's *The Art of War*
Ludwig Wittgenstein's *Philosophical Investigations*

POLITICS

Benedict Anderson's *Imagined Communities*
Aristotle's *Politics*
Bernard Bailyn's *The Ideological Origins of the American Revolution*
Edmund Burke's *Reflections on the Revolution in France*
John C. Calhoun's *A Disquisition on Government*
Ha-Joon Chang's *Kicking Away the Ladder*
Hamid Dabashi's *Iran: A People Interrupted*
Hamid Dabashi's *Theology of Discontent: The Ideological Foundation of the Islamic Revolution in Iran*
Robert Dahl's *Democracy and its Critics*
Robert Dahl's *Who Governs?*
David Brion Davis's *The Problem of Slavery in the Age of Revolution*

The Macat Library By Discipline

Alexis De Tocqueville's *Democracy in America*
James Ferguson's *The Anti-Politics Machine*
Frank Dikotter's *Mao's Great Famine*
Sheila Fitzpatrick's *Everyday Stalinism*
Eric Foner's *Reconstruction: America's Unfinished Revolution, 1863-1877*
Milton Friedman's *Capitalism and Freedom*
Francis Fukuyama's *The End of History and the Last Man*
John Lewis Gaddis's *We Now Know: Rethinking Cold War History*
Ernest Gellner's *Nations and Nationalism*
David Graeber's *Debt: the First 5000 Years*
Antonio Gramsci's *The Prison Notebooks*
Alexander Hamilton, John Jay & James Madison's *The Federalist Papers*
Friedrich Hayek's *The Road to Serfdom*
Christopher Hill's *The World Turned Upside Down*
Thomas Hobbes's *Leviathan*
John A. Hobson's *Imperialism: A Study*
Samuel P. Huntington's *The Clash of Civilizations and the Remaking of World Order*
Tony Judt's *Postwar: A History of Europe Since 1945*
David C. Kang's *China Rising: Peace, Power and Order in East Asia*
Paul Kennedy's *The Rise and Fall of Great Powers*
Robert Keohane's *After Hegemony*
Martin Luther King Jr.'s *Why We Can't Wait*
Henry Kissinger's *World Order: Reflections on the Character of Nations and the Course of History*
John Locke's *Two Treatises of Government*
Niccolò Machiavelli's *The Prince*
Thomas Robert Malthus's *An Essay on the Principle of Population*
Mahmood Mamdani's *Citizen and Subject: Contemporary Africa And The Legacy Of Late Colonialism*
Karl Marx's *Capital*
John Stuart Mill's *On Liberty*
John Stuart Mill's *Utilitarianism*
Hans Morgenthau's *Politics Among Nations*
Thomas Paine's *Common Sense*
Thomas Paine's *Rights of Man*
Thomas Piketty's *Capital in the Twenty-First Century*
Robert D. Putman's *Bowling Alone*
John Rawls's *Theory of Justice*
Jean-Jacques Rousseau's *The Social Contract*
Theda Skocpol's *States and Social Revolutions*
Adam Smith's *The Wealth of Nations*
Sun Tzu's *The Art of War*
Henry David Thoreau's *Civil Disobedience*
Thucydides's *The History of the Peloponnesian War*
Kenneth Waltz's *Theory of International Politics*
Max Weber's *Politics as a Vocation*
Odd Arne Westad's *The Global Cold War: Third World Interventions And The Making Of Our Times*

POSTCOLONIAL STUDIES

Roland Barthes's *Mythologies*
Frantz Fanon's *Black Skin, White Masks*
Homi K. Bhabha's *The Location of Culture*
Gustavo Gutiérrez's *A Theology of Liberation*
Edward Said's *Orientalism*
Gayatri Chakravorty Spivak's *Can the Subaltern Speak?*

PSYCHOLOGY

Gordon Allport's *The Nature of Prejudice*
Alan Baddeley & Graham Hitch's *Aggression: A Social Learning Analysis*
Albert Bandura's *Aggression: A Social Learning Analysis*
Leon Festinger's *A Theory of Cognitive Dissonance*
Sigmund Freud's *The Interpretation of Dreams*
Betty Friedan's *The Feminine Mystique*
Michael R. Gottfredson & Travis Hirschi's *A General Theory of Crime*
Eric Hoffer's *The True Believer: Thoughts on the Nature of Mass Movements*
William James's *Principles of Psychology*
Elizabeth Loftus's *Eyewitness Testimony*
A. H. Maslow's *A Theory of Human Motivation*
Stanley Milgram's *Obedience to Authority*
Steven Pinker's *The Better Angels of Our Nature*
Oliver Sacks's *The Man Who Mistook His Wife For a Hat*
Richard Thaler & Cass Sunstein's *Nudge: Improving Decisions About Health, Wealth and Happiness*
Amos Tversky's *Judgment under Uncertainty: Heuristics and Biases*
Philip Zimbardo's *The Lucifer Effect*

SCIENCE

Rachel Carson's *Silent Spring*
William Cronon's *Nature's Metropolis: Chicago And The Great West*
Alfred W. Crosby's *The Columbian Exchange*
Charles Darwin's *On the Origin of Species*
Richard Dawkin's *The Selfish Gene*
Thomas Kuhn's *The Structure of Scientific Revolutions*
Geoffrey Parker's *Global Crisis: War, Climate Change and Catastrophe in the Seventeenth Century*
Mathis Wackernagel & William Rees's *Our Ecological Footprint*

SOCIOLOGY

Michelle Alexander's *The New Jim Crow: Mass Incarceration in the Age of Colorblindness*
Gordon Allport's *The Nature of Prejudice*
Albert Bandura's *Aggression: A Social Learning Analysis*
Hanna Batatu's *The Old Social Classes And The Revolutionary Movements Of Iraq*
Ha-Joon Chang's *Kicking Away the Ladder*
W. E. B. Du Bois's *The Souls of Black Folk*
Émile Durkheim's *On Suicide*
Frantz Fanon's *Black Skin, White Masks*
Frantz Fanon's *The Wretched of the Earth*
Eric Foner's *Reconstruction: America's Unfinished Revolution, 1863-1877*
Eugene Genovese's *Roll, Jordan, Roll: The World the Slaves Made*
Jack Goldstone's *Revolution and Rebellion in the Early Modern World*
Antonio Gramsci's *The Prison Notebooks*
Richard Herrnstein & Charles A Murray's *The Bell Curve: Intelligence and Class Structure in American Life*
Eric Hoffer's *The True Believer: Thoughts on the Nature of Mass Movements*
Jane Jacobs's *The Death and Life of Great American Cities*
Robert Lucas's *Why Doesn't Capital Flow from Rich to Poor Countries?*
Jay Macleod's *Ain't No Makin' It: Aspirations and Attainment in a Low Income Neighborhood*
Elaine May's *Homeward Bound: American Families in the Cold War Era*
Douglas McGregor's *The Human Side of Enterprise*
C. Wright Mills's *The Sociological Imagination*

The Macat Library By Discipline

Thomas Piketty's *Capital in the Twenty-First Century*
Robert D. Putman's *Bowling Alone*
David Riesman's *The Lonely Crowd: A Study of the Changing American Character*
Edward Said's *Orientalism*
Joan Wallach Scott's *Gender and the Politics of History*
Theda Skocpol's *States and Social Revolutions*
Max Weber's *The Protestant Ethic and the Spirit of Capitalism*

THEOLOGY

Augustine's *Confessions*
Benedict's *Rule of St Benedict*
Gustavo Gutiérrez's *A Theology of Liberation*
Carole Hillenbrand's *The Crusades: Islamic Perspectives*
David Hume's *Dialogues Concerning Natural Religion*
Immanuel Kant's *Religion within the Boundaries of Mere Reason*
Ernst Kantorowicz's *The King's Two Bodies: A Study in Medieval Political Theology*
Søren Kierkegaard's *The Sickness Unto Death*
C. S. Lewis's *The Abolition of Man*
Saba Mahmood's *The Politics of Piety: The Islamic Revival and the Feminist Subject*
Baruch Spinoza's *Ethics*
Keith Thomas's *Religion and the Decline of Magic*

COMING SOON

Chris Argyris's *The Individual and the Organisation*
Seyla Benhabib's *The Rights of Others*
Walter Benjamin's *The Work Of Art in the Age of Mechanical Reproduction*
John Berger's *Ways of Seeing*
Pierre Bourdieu's *Outline of a Theory of Practice*
Mary Douglas's *Purity and Danger*
Roland Dworkin's *Taking Rights Seriously*
James G. March's *Exploration and Exploitation in Organisational Learning*
Ikujiro Nonaka's *A Dynamic Theory of Organizational Knowledge Creation*
Griselda Pollock's *Vision and Difference*
Amartya Sen's *Inequality Re-Examined*
Susan Sontag's *On Photography*
Yasser Tabbaa's *The Transformation of Islamic Art*
Ludwig von Mises's *Theory of Money and Credit*

Macat Disciplines

Access the greatest ideas and thinkers across entire disciplines, including

AFRICANA STUDIES

Chinua Achebe's *An Image of Africa: Racism in Conrad's Heart of Darkness*

W. E. B. Du Bois's *The Souls of Black Folk*

Zora Neale Hurston's *Characteristics of Negro Expression*

Martin Luther King Jr.'s *Why We Can't Wait*

Toni Morrison's *Playing in the Dark: Whiteness in the American Literary Imagination*

Macat analyses are available from all good bookshops and libraries.

Access hundreds of analyses through one, multimedia tool.
Join free for one month **library.macat.com**

Macat Disciplines

Access the greatest ideas and thinkers across entire disciplines, including

FEMINISM, GENDER AND QUEER STUDIES

Simone De Beauvoir's
The Second Sex

Michel Foucault's
History of Sexuality

Betty Friedan's
The Feminine Mystique

Saba Mahmood's
*The Politics of Piety:
The Islamic Revival and
the Feminist Subject*

Joan Wallach Scott's
*Gender and the
Politics of History*

Mary Wollstonecraft's
*A Vindication of the
Rights of Woman*

Virginia Woolf's
A Room of One's Own

Judith Butler's
Gender Trouble

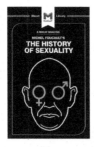